six DANGEROUS QUESTIONS

*to transform
your view
of the world*

paul borthwick

InterVarsity Press
Downers Grove, Illinois

InterVarsity Press® is the book-publishing division of InterVarsity Christian Fellowship®, a student movement active on campus at hundreds of universities, colleges and schools of nursing in the United States of America, and a member movement of the International Fellowship of Evangelical Students. For information about local and regional activities, write Public Relations Dept., InterVarsity Christian Fellowship, 6400 Schroeder Rd., P.O. Box 7895, Madison, WI 53707-7895.

Cover photograph: Tony Stone Images

ISBN 0-8308-1685-2

Printed in the United States of America

Library of Congress Cataloging-in-Publication Data

Borthwick, Paul, 1954-
    Six dangerous questions to transform your view of the world/Paul
Borthwick.
      p.   cm.
    Includes bibliographical references.
    ISBN 0-8308-1685-2 (pbk.: alk. paper)
    1. Christian life. 2. Theology.   I. Title.
BV4501.2.B646 1996
230—dc20
        96-33500
        CIP

20	19	18	17	16	15	14	13	12	11	10	9	8
12	11	10	09	08	07	06	05	04	03			

To Christie,
who faithfully challenges me
to pursue an enlarged vision of God and his world

1
• • • • • •

WHAT'S A WORLDVIEW?

And Elisha prayed, "O LORD,
open his eyes so he may see."
(2 Kings 6:17)

"The United States is having an identity crisis." The bold print
on the full-page advertisement caught my eye. The headline
went on, "24 million Americans can't find our country on a map
of the world."

The statistic shocked me, so I read on. The advertisement was
part of National Geography Awareness Week, and the writers
highlighted the relative lack of world knowledge (especially of
world geography) among Americans.

As a follower of Jesus Christ, I find that geographic knowledge follows my beliefs. My Christian commitment demands
that I be concerned about the world for which Jesus died. Yet I
find that quite a few Christians are no different from the population surveyed for National Geography Awareness Week by the
National Geographic Society. People in our church have told me

that Vietnam is next to Surinam, that Africa is a country and that communism has been eradicated in the world (evidently they forget the People's Republic of China, where over 20 percent of the world's population lives under communist rule).

Many people in the United States of America—regardless of their religious convictions—seem to manifest this lack of global awareness; but to avoid singling out the United States unfairly, we need to acknowledge that many cultures and nations make the same mistake. The ancient dynasties of China named their country "Middle Kingdom," as if they were at the center of the world and all other cultures were peripheral. The Masai people in East Africa believe that God has uniquely chosen them and therefore all the cattle on earth belong to them (which has caused some cattle-rustling problems in the past!). Every culture and ethnicity has its own "center-of-the-world" problems.

Our geographical knowledge problem flows from what sociologists call our *worldview.* Our worldview determines how we look at ourselves, our world and our roles in the world. If our worldview leads us to believe that we (or our people) occupy the center of the universe, we will usually care little for other countries or cultures.

If, on the other hand, we see ourselves as neighbors in the global village or as God's messengers declaring his glory to the nations (Ps 96:3), then world awareness grows as a natural byproduct of our view of the universe. We look at other people and cultures with respect, compassion and a desire to communicate the gospel to them.

Worldview and Behavior

Our worldview determines how we live. Those who assume that they belong to some "master race" try to conquer and subdue all others. Those who believe their village to be the center of the world will evaluate other cultures and communities by what they perceive as normative village life. In contrast, those who assume a submissive or victimization worldview may adapt a mentality that diminishes initiative and an assumption that "everybody else owes me something." In short, how we view the world affects how we act in it.

The principle carries over to our lives as followers of Christ. If we personalize our faith, failing to integrate our life in Christ into life in our world, we may find personal, private comfort, but we will fall short in our Jesus-assigned mission to be "salt" and "light" in the world.

If, on the other hand, we view ourselves as Jesus' agents of change and hope in the world, we discover the motivational foundation for activity in outreach, social service, justice ministry, missions and world evangelization.

Peter Cotterell, former missionary to Ethiopia and now principal of London Bible College, points out that the Christian worldview originates from three major components: our existential awareness of the world (our life experience), our understanding of Scripture and our own self-interest.[1]

Our current tendency in the formation of the Western worldview—even in conservative Christian circles—relies very heavily on components 1 (existential awareness) and 3 (self-interest), often at the expense of component 2 (biblical understanding). The result? "Truth-for-me" replaces Truth, and "how I feel about it" overrules the dogmatic affirmations of Scripture. If we live in a cocoon safely shielded from world poverty, or if we grow self-absorbed with our own needs, we turn our attention away from the world, no matter what the Bible says about the poor or the eternal needs of people outside of Christ.

Consider how Cotterell's three components might affect our responses to the "Six Dangerous Questions" addressed in this book.

1. Who is Jesus?

"My family is Christian" (existential awareness), "and all of my friends are Christian" (self-interest); "therefore, I believe what they say about Jesus" (without any regard for the biblical teaching).

Or, in contrast: "Most of the Christians I know are hypocrites" (existential awareness), "and I've found greater religious experience with the New Age" (self-interest); "therefore, Jesus is at best a great religious teacher and no more" (again, concluded without examination of the biblical or historical records).

2-3. Do I believe in heaven? Do I believe in hell?

"I fear death" (existential awareness), "and I cannot imagine a good God allowing me to go anywhere but heaven" (self-interest); "therefore, I assume that all of the people on earth (except maybe those Hitler-like people who are really bad) are going to heaven" (without an evaluation of the Bible's teaching on either subject).

4. Does Christianity matter?

"I trust in Jesus as my personal Savior" (existential experience), "but I would never offend others by presenting Jesus as the key to the answers to worldwide problems" (self-interest); "so I've decided that my faith applies to my religious life but not to the world around me" (regardless of the biblical call to be salt and light in the world).

5. Do I believe that God wants to use my life?

"I find it so presumptuous when zealous Christians say that 'God wants to use me to change the world' " (existential experience); "I can scarcely manage with my own problems" (self-interest). "I doubt that God wants to use me to change anything—except maybe myself" (a conclusion drawn without a serious consideration of Jesus' call to be his witnesses to the "ends of the earth"—Acts 1:8).

6. Whose agenda will I live by?

"I have lots of plans for my own life" (self-interest), "and I got really messed up when my parents tried to control my life" (existential awareness); "so I think the best thing is to plan out my own agenda for life" (without trying to make Jesus my Lord as the Bible affirms).

Sam Wilson and Gordon Aeschliman, in their book *The Hidden Half,* push us a step further on this issue of a biblical worldview:

Anthropologists explain that at our cores is a basic view of reality—a worldview. That worldview determines who we are, what we value, and how we behave.

If our worldview is unChristian, or less-than-biblical, it will inevitably surface in values and actions that contradict the heart of the biblical worldview.

But if my actions stem from a biblical worldview, then it becomes a matter of faithful obedience. I can allow a fad to slip away, but not something that goes as deep as obedience. I have decided to follow Jesus with my whole life, and I understand where he's going. It's no longer a matter of choosing a career or lifestyle—it's a matter of faithfulness.[2]

Worldview Implications

Getting God's view of the world would challenge the natural, self-serving instincts reflected in the less-than-biblical responses to the Six Dangerous Questions. We choose to narrow our vision of the world because a narrower vision means narrower responsibilities and fewer challenging involvements. A narrow and unbiblical worldview allows us to maintain our stereotypes, use God for our own purposes and stay detached from much of our world.

With a narrow, self-serving worldview, we can close our eyes to world realities:

□ we can live selfish lives without regard for the millions of poor or the 1 billion people in our world who go to bed hungry every night;

□ we can forget about 100 million street children in the world, living in danger in cities like Rio de Janeiro, Calcutta, Manila, New York and Bangkok;

□ we can pretend that the Western church leads the Christian world—when in reality the modern Christian movement finds its world center in Latin America, Asia and Africa;

□ we can think that speaking out about our Christian faith is not necessary because "everyone has had the chance to hear about Jesus"—when in reality there are millions in our world who know nothing about the good news of life and forgiveness in Jesus Christ.

Natural Instincts

The biblical account of Jonah illustrates the instinctive human response to an enlarged worldview. Jonah was raised to hate the Ninevites (and probably to wish God's condemnation on them). From his vantage point the Ninevites were violent pagans, cannibals deserving God's wrath. When God called Jonah to go to Nineveh (Jon 1:2), Jonah ran the other direction. His existential awareness and self-interest overruled God's word to him.

In our telling of this Bible story, we often paint Jonah as a coward who ran from confrontation, but this portrayal contradicts the biblical account. Jonah had good reason to fear the Ninevites: they had a reputation for extraordinary violence and ferocity, and it would frighten most prophets to go to such people to declare God's judgment.

The later chapters of the book of Jonah reveal that Jonah did not run because he was a coward. Jonah reveals that he ran to Tarshish because he did not want God's mercy to be poured out on his enemies. Seeing the Ninevites saved from judgment did not fit with Jonah's view of himself, his culture or the world. Up to this point Jonah had lived as a racist who wanted the mercies of God exclusively for himself and his people (and certainly not for his enemies the Ninevites). He ran from preaching to the Ninevites because he knew that he would be representing a "gracious and compassionate God, slow to anger and abounding in love, a God who relents from sending calamity" (4:2).

Jonah's worldview led him to hate the thought of these Ninevites being recipients of God's mercy. When God acts compassionately toward them (3:10), Jonah despairs to the point of suicide. God has radically challenged Jonah's worldview, and Jonah whines, "Now, O LORD, take away my life, for it is better for me to die than to live" (4:3). Translation: "God, I would rather die than try to see the world (and these people from Nineveh) with your eyes of compassion. You, Lord, did not act in a way that fits my worldview, so I want to quit life."

Jonah's response illustrates why I call my six questions "dangerous": the answers may threaten many of the preconceived ideas we have about God, about life and about our world.

Isolationism?

The same natural instinct that Jonah displayed is apparent today in the church around the world. In the Fall 1995 issue of

Leadership magazine, the editors posited that a major trend in the church in the United States is that "church members are more near sighted." They explained,

In general, Americans are moving from being globally to locally minded. This trend seems counter-intuitive, given all the talk about our world being a global village. But America in general and the church in particular seem to be circling the wagons.

Some examples of this shift in the church: Denominations are having trouble replacing retiring missionaries; prayer movements are focused more on spiritual renewal in America than on world evangelism; giving to foreign missions is declining.[3]

The problem is not unique in the United States. Around the world, this local-versus-global orientation expresses itself in the daily life of the church.

□ *Financial commitments*. A church raises thousands of dollars to help flood victims in the midwestern United States (all of whom will benefit from government aid) while neglecting the victims of awesome floods devastating Bangladesh. A church leader in India says, "We'll support local concerns only because the needs are so great here at home," without regard for needs beyond his own city and culture and country.

□ *Involvement*. A Haitian pastor observes that he has never crossed the mountain to share the gospel with the next village because his call is local. An American woman explains that she cannot be involved in world missions because God has called her to be committed to the right-to-life movement. When I explain that abortion is a global issue and that her convictions should at least motivate her to pray for China (where abortion and the infanticide of baby girls may reach into the millions annually), she refuses to respond.

□ *Prayer.* We pray for local concerns or national issues exclusively. If we go international, it's to remember our own national concerns overseas. Our locally bound prayers imply that God is some sort of local or national deity, rather than Lord of the nations and Supreme Head of the global church to which we belong.

Responding to this trend toward insulating ourselves from the world, Leith Anderson, a globally aware pastor from the Minneapolis area, challenges the church in the United States and beyond, asking if we are going to mimic the "our-nation-first" sentiment that is growing in the world. Documenting what he calls our "isolationist roots," he points to trends that turned American interests inward.

A shift outward occurred after World War II. Anderson observes that after we entered the war, "overnight the popular culture changed from isolationism to militarism. When the war ended in 1945, militarism turned into unprecedented internationalism." The American church followed suit and sent huge numbers of missionaries; in fact, the United States became the primary sending nation in the modern missionary movement.

After the start of glasnost and détente in 1980, Anderson says, we started shifting inward again. Rising crime at home, government problems and a declining economy started to take priority over helping other nations. Our involvement internationally became based on "American interests" rather than justice or anything close to biblical concerns for righteousness.

Anderson concludes that our culture again has slipped into an isolationist position, and he asks if we will adopt a worldview based on our limited experience and self-interest or the worldview that God advocates for us in the Scriptures:

The question for Christians at the end of the twentieth century is: Will we become counter-cultural? Will we follow the Great Commission of Acts 1:8 [to be Christ's witnesses in Jerusalem, Judea, Samaria, and to the utmost ends of the earth] more than the cultural trend of the 90's?[4]

Why Are We Doing This?

I sat at a circle of tables with about twenty-five missions pastors from large North American churches. Each man or woman represented a church with over one thousand members and a missions budget of over $500,000. We were together for three days of open discussion, with no predetermined agenda.

The group facilitator asked, "Does anyone have any questions or issues that you'd like us to address in these next few days?"

After a few moments of silence, I raised my hand. "I'd like us to address the question 'Why are we doing this?' "

"Why we are meeting together?" the facilitator responded.

"No. Why do we advocate global missions? Why do our churches allocate millions of dollars to crosscultural outreach? Why are we trying to stir the world vision of our parishioners?"

The others seemed a little dumbfounded by the question, so I went on: "Are we promoting world missions just to follow the trend toward the 'global village'? Are we sending hundreds of people to Russia because that's where they are called and needed, or because we're following some American ideal of defeating Russian communism? If the foreign policy of the United States is to pull back and diminish our presence in the world, will the church follow—or are we operating on Jesus' foreign policy? Are we doing short-term missions simply because it's great experiential education or because it actually contributes to the worldwide growth of the church of Jesus Christ?"

By this time some were saying "amen." Others scratched their heads, thinking my questions irrelevant. Some got defensive, thinking I was attacking their programs. I was merely asking us to reconsider: What are the foundations of our involvement in the world? What's our biblical worldview, and how do we live it out in the world through our churches?

Retreat or Advance?

The church shrinks back from involvement in the world. Global and geographic knowledge declines. Some fear genuine interaction with the secularized world we live in. Many focus on the "needs right here at home" and retreat from considering the world beyond our own culture or country. We spend our prayers, our time and our financial resources on local concerns—often at the expense of the complex, needy world beyond our borders. At the core of our retreat is our worldview—how we view God, ourselves and our roles in this world.

We can choose to retreat into the safety of a narrow worldview, or we can enter the danger zone by addressing Six Dangerous Questions. Our answers will determine whether we advance as forward-looking Christians committed to positive change or retreat as Christians withdrawing from the world God calls us to affect.

2
• • • • • • •

WORLDVIEW & CROSSCULTURAL INVOLVEMENT

Then Peter began to speak: "I
now realize how true it
is that God does not show
favoritism but accepts men from
every nation who fear
him and do what is right."
(Acts 10:34-35)

While my wife and I were traveling through India, we received a copy of *The Hindu,* an English-language newspaper. An editorial headline caught my eye: "Globalization and Culture." *Globalization* is one of my favorite terms; to me, it speaks of the creation of global interdependence, greater crosscultural understanding and technology that serves international dialogue.

The author, K. N. Panikkar of the Jawaharlal Nehru University in New Delhi, had a far less favorable opinion. Here's how his editorial started:

Words often disguise what they really mean, particularly when they form part of an ideological effort in the pursuit of hegemony. Globalization is such a word which is a euphemism for domination. It suggests something entirely different from what it actually attempts to achieve. When innocently interpreted, it represents an ideal process of equal sharing and voluntary participation. Yet, it needs no ingenuity to discern that any relationship in the contemporary global order of uneven development cannot but be unequal.[1]

Thereafter he launched into an articulate description of how economic globalization has become "a new era of conquest" for capitalist forces. He asserts that references to "modern society" represent the interest of an elite minority and that the exportation of McDonald's, Kentucky Fried Chicken and Levis has little positive impact on the 62 percent of Bombay's population living in huts and on the streets. To Panikkar, globalization "only ensures the necessary climate for domination and hegemonisation by the consortium of world capitalist countries."[2]

The article reflected one tragic truth about human civilization: the propensity we have to exploit others (or exercise superiority over others) for our own benefit. Such exploitation has no place in the formation of a biblical worldview. Whether we refer to economic domination (as did Panikkar) or to cultural domination, we must repent and turn from exploitation if we are to become true representatives of Christ.

Battling Ethnocentrism

Nothing undermines the effective communication of the gospel of Jesus Christ as much as ethnocentrism, which the dictionary defines as "the belief in the superiority of one's own ethnic group." I will use the term here more broadly, to refer as well to belief in the superiority of one's own nation, culture and political system. We must accept the sad legacy of well-meaning missionaries in the past who added culturally imperialistic baggage to the message of the gospel, but we can grow past their failures.

The gospel that we proclaim does come with standards that transcend culture (that is, commands that must be obeyed no matter how "culturally acceptable" a behavior or practice has become). Converted liars cannot remain liars; headhunters cannot remain headhunters; the sexually promiscuous must repent and change. At the same time, our desire as followers of Jesus Christ is to promote him, not our cultural or ethnic practices. If our worldview emanates from ethnocentric thinking, our ability to share the love of Christ across cultures and our freedom to participate in the worldwide body of Christ will be hampered.

Ethnocentrism is our common enemy, manifesting itself (however subtly) in a variety of forms across and within cultures:

☐ our world maps, which put the developed world at the center and the less-developed world on the "bottom"

☐ our assumption that everyone who is intelligent should speak and write our language

☐ the tendency to judge other cultures by our own standards—for example, Americans' propensity to say, "People in England drive on the *wrong* side of the road"

☐ speaking in exaggerated terms about our own nation—"ours is the greatest nation on earth"—without regard either for the statement's truthfulness or for how that statement might affect our neighbors

☐ expecting people of other ethnicities to adapt to our cultural styles without our adapting to theirs

☐ making insulting statements or creating stereotypes to cover our own inadequacies—"You people always have such funny names," or "Why would intelligent people choose chopsticks over a fork?" or "Don't you folks ever start and end your meetings on time?"

When we get to the Six Dangerous Questions, we want to be pursuing a biblical worldview that transcends our ethnocentric tendencies. As we grow toward that end, it is helpful to realize that believers in biblical times struggled with this issue as well.

The Church Confronts Ethnocentrism: Three Examples

Perhaps the greatest transformation of worldviews in the Bible occurs in the Acts account of the disciples and the early church. Up until the crucifixion, and even after the resurrection, the disciples maintained their ethnocentrism. Despite several years of walking with Jesus and observing his outreach to Gentiles and Samaritans as well as Jews, the disciples still had their eyes on Jesus as the political messiah who would defeat the Romans and return their people to power. After Jesus' resurrection, the disciples demonstrated their nationalistic desire: "When they met together, they asked him, 'Lord, are you at this time going to restore the kingdom to Israel?' " (Acts 1:6).

Jesus' reply to their question set in motion a gigantic paradigm shift that would require these ethnocentric disciples to break out of their old worldview.

Example 1—Acts 1:8

Jesus does not answer the disciples' question about establishing the kingdom in Israel. Instead he gives his disciples a command that would break through every level of their ethnocentrism: "You will receive power when the Holy Spirit comes on you; and you will be my witnesses in Jerusalem, and in all Judea and Samaria, and to the ends of the earth" (Acts 1:8).

Then Jesus gives no opportunity for objection or reply; he ascends into heaven, leaving his eleven remaining disciples with an *I-wonder-what-he-meant-by-that* confusion, "looking intently up into the sky" (1:10).

With the command of Acts 1:8, Jesus began the process of expanding the worldview of his disciples. He identifies three basic principles—basic for them and for us—that must be present as we later ask the six dangerous questions that will challenge our views of the world.

Principle 1: Our power comes from the Holy Spirit. Ethnocentrism (as well as racism, sexism and other means of lifting ourselves up at someone else's expense) goes so deep into our character that only the awesome power of God's Holy Spirit can excise it. If we sincerely desire to look at and respond in love to a world full of challenge and diversity, we must ask for the Holy Spirit to give us the power to change.

Principle 2: Our presence is as witnesses. God does not send us into the world as cultural imperialists; there is no room for feelings of ethnic, cultural or national superiority. We go as his witnesses, and we testify that what he has done for us in Christ is available to all who will respond to his love.

Principle 3: Our challenge is the world. Jesus commissions his disciples to go to

☐ Jerusalem, the place of their failure and denial only weeks before

☐ Judea, the country that rejected Jesus as Messiah

☐ Samaria, land of ethnic hostilities and historical hatred

☐ the ends of the earth, far outside their comfort zone, the place of great unknowns

Jesus' call to be his witnesses covers not only a geographic expansion of distance but also a progression across cultural, ethnic and linguistic barriers. If I had been standing with Jesus that day, I think I would have agreed to be a witness to my friends and family. I might have consented to attempt to bring the good news to my fellow Israelites. But to Samaria and the ends of the earth? No way!

The book of Acts ignites with this commission, which starts the process of breaking the disciples and the church out of ethnocentricity.

Example 2—Acts 8

The command of Acts 1:8 seems clear—the gospel should be preached to the whole world, starting in Jerusalem and rippling out across geographic and ethnic barriers: to Judea, Samaria and the ends of the earth. But seven chapters later the church is still locked into an ethnocentric model. The believers have received the Holy Spirit's power, and they have witnessed with boldness, but they have stayed in Jerusalem.

That early church did what we all do: they started out as risk-takers and pioneers, and then they got settled. Perhaps they got too comfortable. So God intervenes to launch them out again: "On that day a great persecution broke out against the church at Jerusalem, and all except the apostles were scattered throughout Judea and Samaria" (Acts 8:1).

Phases two and three of the Acts 1:8 commission get under way because the church is thrust out by hardship and persecution. Pain and suffering, the death of Stephen and the imprisonment of other believers now focus the church on its primary mission.

Philip emerges as the star of Acts 8. He demonstrates the power of the Holy Spirit promised in Acts 1:8 (see Acts 8:6-7). He goes out as a witness—first to Samaritans, then to an Ethiopian, then to the people in Azotus and finally all the way to Caesarea. And he introduces the gospel to people in Samaria and the ends of the earth.

Philip demonstrates a key principle in the process of worldview transformation: he is *available* to God. First he finds himself in Samaria, and he "proclaimed the Christ there" (8:5). Then he goes south to Gaza, where he meets the Ethiopian eunuch (who is racially and socioeconomically different from Philip), and Philip "told him the good news about Jesus" (v. 35). Then the Spirit of God beams Philip over to Azotus, and we find him "preaching the gospel in all the towns until he reached Caesarea" (v. 40).

Philip's availability transcended his ethnocentricity. Philip was more concerned about proclaiming the gospel than about his own nationalistic pride or fears. His availability illustrates the powerful way that God will work through a person who allows God to reshape his or her worldview.

Missionaries get excited at the thought of being the first to introduce an ethnic group or a language group to the gospel. Even greater is the privilege of introducing a nation to the gospel. But Philip exceeded all of these: he introduced a continent to the gospel! Philip made himself available to be used by God outside his own ethnocentric boxes, and God used him to introduce a continent to the gospel, by introducing the first African to Jesus Christ.

Example 3—Acts 10

It took persecution to break the church out of Jerusalem into Judea and Samaria in Acts 8, but it took a vision and three dreams to get the church to start after those whom Jewish believers saw as representing the "ends of the earth"—the Gentiles.

Acts 10 tells the story of two men whose worldviews changed as they saw God's perspective beyond their ethnic limitations. For the Gentile Cornelius, the transformation of his worldview meant understanding that God has no limitations dictated by race or ethnic origin. For Peter, the Jew who thought that his people had a unique and superior place in the gospel, the transformation of his worldview brought humility and a realization "that God does not show favoritism but accepts men from every nation who fear him and do what is right" (vv. 34-35).

Through the miraculous (visions and dreams) and the mundane (the sharing of a meal), God changed the worldviews of both of these men. Thus the church began to learn that the commission of Acts 1:8 was designed so that all peoples might have the opportunity to respond to Jesus Christ.

The Lesson for Us

From the people in the book of Acts and from a Hindu professor in New Delhi, we learn that we all tend toward ethnocentrism. We want the world to fit into our boxes; we want to evaluate others by our own cultural, economic and ethnic standards. We need the power of God's Holy Spirit at work in us if we are to break out of our ethnocentrism so that we can be his witnesses.

As we get ready to confront the Six Dangerous Questions, we understand that God's transformation of our worldview will be the foundation for our ability to communicate the love of Christ across cultures.

If we see ourselves as neighbors in the global village or as God's messengers declaring his glory to the nations (Ps 96:3), then our worldview will provoke both awareness of and involvement in our world, starting with our neighbors and rippling out to the "ends of the earth." We will look beyond our own ethnocentricity so that we can respond to other people and cultures with respect, desiring to communicate the gospel to them in terms they understand.

3
● ● ● ● ● ● ●

THE SEPARATION OF INTELLECT & LIFESTYLE

Jesus replied: "Love the Lord your God with all your heart and with all your soul and with all your mind."
(Matthew 22:37)

How can we who profess to follow Jesus Christ develop a global worldview, so that we start to look at our world the way God wants us to? Does it mean buying a world map, taking a crosscultural trip or reaching out to an international friend?

Any of those actions could help, but they still do not get to the root of the problem. Actions may change our experiences, but we need to go deeper. We need to wrestle at the philosophical and theological level with the questions that are at the core of our worldview and our lifestyle.

Six Dangerous Questions aims to help us see what we really believe—the convictions that make up our worldview—and then ask whether we need to change our beliefs to bring them in line with the worldview taught to us in the Scriptures.

Time to Integrate

What do we really believe? We have a problem in modern (or what some call postmodern) society with the matter of belief. We use the term in so many ways it has become almost meaningless. We *believe* our team can win the championship; we *believe* facts in science; we *believe* the statistical data from surveys; some of us *believe* in angels and crystals; others claim to *believe* theological truths.

But modern use of *believe* often makes no demands on our lifestyles and priorities. "I believe" has no apparent implications for the way I live. In other words, there is no integration of belief and practice. Belief can take place in my mind while remaining disconnected from the priorities I choose and the life I lead. Consider one example.

A couple entered my office hoping that I would agree to perform their wedding. They were involved at church and in Sunday school; they had completed our church's preengagement class; she had been recently baptized. They gave every impression of being a growing couple desirous of serving God.

As we went through some perfunctory details to begin planning their wedding, it became evident that they were living together as if they were already married. If they had been new believers acting out of ignorance, I would have given them the benefit of the doubt. But when I confronted them with the biblical teaching on purity and virginity before marriage, they said they knew they were living in contradiction to God's Word. They went on to explain their reasoning: God had given them permission to live this way because they were going to get married anyhow.

I told them that without repentance and a lifestyle change, I could not perform their wedding. They left the office upset with my rigidity.

This couple illustrates the dangerous separation that easily creeps into our Christian faith: the ever-increasing distance between intellectual belief and daily, practical issues of lifestyle. The couple would unhesitatingly declare their belief in Jesus as their Savior and Lord, but when confronted with a matter of clear obedience to the lordship of Christ, they chose to remain in a sinful lifestyle. They resisted integrating their faith into this area of their lives.

We all might find it easy to condemn this couple, but be careful. Most of us live with the tension of not having fully integrated our beliefs into the way we live. We say we believe the Ten Commandments, but we lie, use God's name with irreverence, "kill" people with our angry words (according to Jesus' interpretation in Matthew 5) and consistently put career or family or success as idols in the place of God.

Peter Cotterell addresses the matter of integrating our faith thus: "To know a truth is to act on that truth, and to fail to act is to demonstrate a failure of knowledge. Truth must be rescued from its arid isolation in propositional theology, and must be transferred to the arena of everyday living."[1]

Praxis

Liberation theologians introduced the wider Christian community to *praxis,* the idea that our beliefs and our worldviews do not really matter unless they are expressed in practice. No practice = no belief.

Cotterell explains how true praxis (in this case related to the evangelization of the lost) gets nullified as our selfish interests overrule our need to live out our faith. He says that the majority of us don't act on our belief that people are "lost" because our theoretical beliefs are undermined by our self-interest. What we say we believe does not match what we actually do.

The real worldview of an individual is clearly evidenced by his praxis. Millions of Christians profess a concern for those they would theoretically designate the "lost," and the theoretical worldview associated with that concern should lead to their taking steps to reach these lost. That the vast majority take no such steps is because the theoretical worldview is seriously modified by self-interest, producing a praxeologically determinative worldview which would probably not be verbalized by the individual concerned, nor, indeed, acknowledged if it were verbalized by another person.[2]

Jesus challenges us toward praxis when in some of his concluding words to his disciples, he says, "If you love me, you will obey what I command" (Jn 14:15), and again, "If anyone loves me, he will obey my teaching" (14:23). Jesus rebuked those who refused to integrate belief and practice with the question "Why do you call me, 'Lord, Lord,' and do not do what I say?" (Lk 6:46).

James exhorts his readers to praxis when he writes, "Do not merely listen to the word, and so deceive yourselves. Do what it says" (Jas 1:22). He elaborates in chapter 2, explaining that "faith by itself, if it is not accompanied by action, is dead" (v. 17).

Tony Campolo rebukes the church for the drift away from praxis when he observes,

Ironically, even our churches give us the message—spoken or unspoken—that radical sacrifice for the poor and disengagement from the culturally prescribed lifestyle are not really necessary for Christian discipleship. We have reduced being a Christian to agreement with some doctrinal propositions and have ignored the call to radically sacrifice in the name of Christ for the poor and the oppressed.[3]

The six questions taken up in this book are designed to stir us to integrated praxis in our lifestyle, values and view of the world.

The Challenge

A promotional piece for the Urbana 96 missionary conference splashed "Dare to have your worldview challenged" across the top of the page. The letter went on to say, "Urbana 96 is for people who love Jesus and want to . . . ask hard questions and re-evaluate their worldview."

This same challenge comes to me and you, the reader. Consider the Six Dangerous Questions and reevaluate your worldview.

Are you ready to expand your view of the world? Then work through these six questions. In the chapters that follow you will find my attempts to articulate my answers and explain how I try to live in light of my answers.

But let me encourage you: struggle with these questions yourself. Don't just give the pat answer or the answer you learned in catechism class or Sunday school. Don't parrot the answer your Bible study leader or pastor wants. Wrestle with these questions for yourself, with your Bible and your heart open. Allow them to be truly dangerous to you. How we answer and live out these questions will transform our lives.

What are *your* answers?

4

• • • • • • •

Dangerous Question #1

WHO IS JESUS?

*"But what about you?" he
asked. "Who do you say I am?"*
(Matthew 16:15)

"Who is Jesus?" stands alone as the most important theological
and objective question in forming our view of the world, ourselves and our roles in the world. In the Bible the question
appears repeatedly.

☐ Jesus asked it of his disciples: "Who do you say I am?" (Mt
16:15).

☐ The disciples asked it of each other: "They were terrified
and asked each other, 'Who is this? Even the wind and the waves
obey him!' " (Mk 4:41).

☐ The religious leaders asked it of Jesus: "Tell us if you are
the Christ, the Son of God" (Mt 26:63; also Lk 22:67).

☐ Pilate asked it of Jesus: "Are you the king of the Jews?"
(Lk 23:3).

☐ Saul (later Paul) asked it after being blinded on the road to Damascus: "Who are you, Lord?" (Acts 9:5).

To some the question "Who is Jesus?" sounds too basic, but it is the hinge question on which everything else swings.

The answer to this question determines our sense of mission in the world and our outlook on all people (religious or not) who do not follow Jesus Christ. The answer motivates our witness or allows us to drop Jesus into the "just another great religious teacher" slot.

If I conclude that Jesus Christ is simply one possible answer on the multiple-choice test of religious options, then I can find peace in him as my Savior, but I have no sense of urgency to tell anyone else about him. Any sense of praying for or preaching the gospel to those who have never heard of Jesus (Rom 15:20) will be lost.

If we look at Jesus as one among many potential "saviors," we will not comprehend a worldview built on the uniqueness of Jesus (which teaches that there is salvation through Christ alone). Without that conviction we cannot understand what drove missionary pioneers like Hudson Taylor to the interior of China, David Brainerd to evangelize Native Americans, Amy Carmichael to serve children of India and Cameron Townsend to the rigors of Bible translation. Each of these went forth to proclaim the gospel at great personal sacrifice because he or she believed that Jesus alone can offer salvation.

An Age of Pluralism

Colin and I found ourselves next to each other on a flight from Denver to Boston. We chatted about the weather and then got to the "so what do you do?" questions. He was fascinated to meet me, a real-life pastor in a Bible-believing church (I think he had assumed that people like me existed only in museums and novels). We started talking about truth.

Colin's worldview was built on several assumptions. He assumed that all religions are equally valid. He believed that contradictions between religious belief systems are fully acceptable because absolute truth does not exist. He assumed that truths actually exist in parallels, so there is no need for exclusivity. And he understood that the linear, exclusive truth about Jesus is a result of a rationalistic Western worldview.

In contrast, I pointed out, the idea of *one* God and exclusive truth came from Middle Eastern thinking:

☐ Exodus 20:3—God will not tolerate other gods

☐ Isaiah 42:8 and 48:11—God will not share his glory with another (not because God is egomaniacal, but because he is Truth, and giving glory to anything or anyone other than the one true God would be a lie)

☐ Isaiah 43:11—"apart from me there is no savior"

☐ Isaiah 45:23 and Philippians 2:5-11—at his name every knee will bow

When I introduced Colin to the idea that our belief in the uniqueness of Jesus as Absolute Truth is built on the Old Testament affirmation that there is only one God and he alone should be worshiped, he admitted that he had never really investigated biblical Christianity or its Old Testament roots.

Colin reflects pluralism. The spirit of the age believes that all belief systems are valid—except a belief system that affirms anything as *absolute* truth. In short, today's Western worldview is built on pluralism and universalism.

As Colin and I talked, he raised a host of excellent questions. He asked, "But isn't believing in Jesus as the only truth a little belligerent—or at least arrogant? Doesn't it promote a type of religious cultural imperialism?"

I agreed that it could, and I conceded that any proponent of absolute truth can be seen as being belligerent. I also observed that Christians have abused this truth, taking it as liberty to mistreat other cultures and ridicule other religions. I explained that our belief in Jesus as Savior should never be a license to repeat the same mistakes. I tried to show Colin that a Christian worldview is neither belligerent nor imperialistic; rather, we are committed to a person who said, "I am the truth." We recognize that God's truth may show itself in many arenas (what theologians call "general revelation"), but that Jesus is the ultimate expression of God's truth.

Pluralism Hits the Church

My cotraveler Colin never attends church and would never call himself a Christian, yet his pluralistic spirit can be found today throughout the church, even the so-called evangelical church.

Actively, it is seen in those who adhere to what Robertson McQuilkin calls the "New Universalism," the belief that Christ died for sinners and all will be saved on the basis of Christ's provision.[1] In the domain of Roman Catholic theology, Karl Rahner introduced this concept in his theorizing about "anonymous Christians."

Further, McQuilkin sees some of our churches advocating what he calls the "Wider Hope" theory. According to this theory, not all will be saved, but many who have not heard of or responded to Jesus Christ will still be saved, because God is just and will not condemn the sincere seeker after truth (the corollary here is that only those who actively reject the gospel will be lost). Commenting on this, McQuilkin observes, "The problem is that if sincerity saves in religion, it is the only realm in which it saves.

It does not save in science; it does not save in drinking arsenic sincerely believing it was Coke."[2]

The research of James Davison Hunter, documented in his book *Evangelicalism: The Coming Generation,* revealed the active drift away from historical convictions in evangelicalism and toward pluralistic thinking. His studies showed that a significant number of students (almost one-third) in Christian colleges and seminaries were uncertain about the uniqueness of Christ.

> Approximately two-thirds of those surveyed held the traditional view that "the only hope for Heaven is through personal relationship with Jesus Christ." One out of three, however, held the view that "the only hope for Heaven is through personal faith in Jesus Christ except for those who have not had the opportunity to hear of Jesus Christ." The difference between these perspectives is, from the perspective of historical orthodoxy, very important. Those holding to the latter imply that some form of alternative arrangement is provided for those not exposed to the truths of Christianity. God's dealings with the unevangelized are somehow different from his dealings with those who have heard.[3]

The active push in the church toward pluralism and away from belief in salvation through Christ alone is passively complemented in fewer people and financial resources committed to missions to unreached peoples, diminished interest in evangelism, and increased hesitancy to proclaim the absolute truth of Jesus to those of other religions.

What Does the Bible Affirm?

This book builds on the presupposition that we will evaluate our own worldview against the teachings of the Bible, so let's rephrase this chapter's question: "What does the Bible teach about the uniqueness of Jesus?"

The Old Testament foundation starts with Deuteronomy 6:4, known as the *Shema:* "Hear, O Israel: the LORD our God, the LORD is one." This critical statement is expanded throughout the Old Testament (refer above to the Old Testament verses I shared with Colin) to get one basic truth across: there is only one true God, and this God alone should be worshiped. Idolatry is condemned. Worshiping multiple gods is condemned. Total submission to the one and only God is the benchmark of the person of faith. The Old Testament speaks of a unique and exclusive God who reveals himself uniquely in the person of Jesus Christ in the New Testament.

The New Testament witness, originally addressed to people in the syncretistic, pluralistic culture of the Greco-Roman world, built on the Old Testament assumption that there is one true God who has chosen to communicate with his people. In the New Testament, God's ultimate communication takes place in Jesus:

> In the beginning was the Word, and the Word was with God, and the Word was God. He was with God in the beginning. . . . The Word became flesh and made his dwelling among us. We have seen his glory, the glory of the One and Only, who came from the Father, full of grace and truth. . . . No one has ever seen God, but God the One and Only, who is at the Father's side, has made him known. (Jn 1:1-2, 14, 18)

Throughout the New Testament the uniqueness of Jesus is affirmed as the writers present him as God's one and only Messiah, the Savior, the "Lamb [or sacrifice] of God, who takes away the sin of the world" (Jn 1:29).

The writer of Hebrews identifies Jesus as the supreme communication of God:

In the past God spoke to our forefathers through the prophets at many times and in various ways, but in these last days he has spoken to us by his Son, whom he appointed heir of all things, and through whom he made the universe. The Son is the radiance of God's glory and the exact representation of his being, sustaining all things by his powerful word. (Heb 1:1-3)

John 14:6, Acts 4:12 and 1 Timothy 2:5-6 provide the most stunning declarations concerning the uniqueness of Jesus as God's one and only Savior for humankind. In John 14:6 Jesus claims that there is no route back to God except through his person: "I am the way and the truth and the life. No one comes to the Father except through me."

In the book of Acts the apostles affirm Jesus' uniqueness to religious leaders who desired to earn salvation through their own merit and good deeds: "Salvation is found in no one else, for there is no other name under heaven given to men by which we must be saved" (Acts 4:12).

In his first letter to Timothy, Paul points to Jesus as the only bridge between the holy God and fallen humanity, Jesus Christ the mediator: "For there is one God and one mediator between God and men, the man Christ Jesus, who gave himself as a ransom for all men—the testimony given in its proper time" (1 Tim 2:5-6).

Some see these verses as selective prooftexts used at the expense of other New Testament teachings. Peter Cotterell of London Bible College answers this accusation, referring to John 14:6 and Acts 4:12:

Although these two verses of the New Testament are in a sense isolated verses, they are entirely in accord with the New Testament teaching in general. They cannot be dismissed as mere eccentricities. It simply will not do to import into the Bible the modern reluctance to believe in absolutes. We may decide to reject absolutes ourselves, but we must do that for ourselves and by ourselves. We cannot claim biblical support for our decisions.[4]

The resurrection provides us with the most tangible and physical evidence for the uniqueness of Christ. Craig Blomberg writes, "No religion stands or falls with a claim about the resurrection of its founder the way that Christianity does."[5] The resurrection establishes Jesus' claims to lordship and demonstrates his power over death and the grave. From his stance as resurrected Lord, Jesus issues the "Great Commission" in Matthew. Before sending his disciples out to make disciples of all nations, he begins, "All authority in heaven and on earth has been given to me . . ." (Mt 28:18). The resurrection sets Jesus apart from all others, and so he declares that he has all authority—over all other gods, all other religions, all other systems of salvation. He alone stands risen from the dead to save us and send us out. And he does send us out!

Listen again to Cotterell:

From the first post-resurrection appearances of Jesus the Christian Church has been of its essence a missionary Church. . . . There was salvation in Jesus and nowhere else. There was no salvation to be found in the plethora of religions on offer around the Mediterranean basin. Gods constructed by human hands were no gods at all. The Christians were confident that in Christ God had not merely spoken to all humanity: he had himself come among them with the ultimate authoritative response to the human condition.[6]

The witness of Scripture is that salvation is found nowhere else. Therefore people outside of Christ's saving power have no hope of salvation. The harshness of this must dig deep into our souls—people (even the sincere, the religious, the moral) are lost without Jesus—as we wrestle with the question "Who is Jesus?"

Robertson McQuilkin tangles with this tough conclusion in *The Great Omission:*

> We may not be able to prove from Scripture with absolute certainty that no soul since Pentecost has ever been saved by extraordinary means without the knowledge of Christ. But neither can we prove from Scripture that a single soul has been so saved. If there is an alternative [to Jesus], God has not told us of it. If God in His revelation felt it mandatory not to proffer such a hope, how much more should we refrain from theorizing. . . . So long as the truth revealed to us identifies only one way of escape, this is what we must live by and proclaim.[7]

In short, if there's another way of salvation outside of Jesus Christ, God has not told us what it is.

If Jesus Is the Truth . . .

If Jesus alone is the truth and no one can find salvation apart from him, what are the implications for us in living out this aspect of our worldview?

1. Urgency: we have a Savior to proclaim. If Jesus is the only Savior, then our sense of compulsion to preach the gospel increases. We find ourselves imitating Paul, who said, "Woe to me if I do not preach the gospel!" (1 Cor 9:16).

I admit that although for a long time I professed to believe that Jesus is "the only way," I didn't feel much compulsion to preach or proclaim Jesus to others. Until I started traveling to other lands and observing people of other faiths.

In Trinidad, then Nepal and later India, I saw Hindu people

in total sincerity and even desperation bowing down to inanimate statues of animals, multiheaded deities and carved statues in hopes of appeasing the inevitable condemnation of karma.

In North Africa and Indonesia, I saw diligent Muslims in total submission to a God who does not reply, acts capriciously and does not make himself known.

In Thailand, Hong Kong, China and Myanmar (Burma), I encountered Buddhists bowing down, repeating prayers and burning incense to please golden statues who could not and will not reply.

Returning to my own culture from these international experiences, I was suddenly and keenly aware of people devoted to other false ideologies right around me—people living lifestyles dedicated to materialism, intellectualism, narcissism and eroticism.

These trips made me eager to declare Jesus to all who do not know him, not just those in foreign lands. According to the Scriptures, people are lost based on their lack of relationship with Jesus Christ, not on their geography. The first people God calls us to reach out to are those right around us.

Seeing lostness compels us to proclaim the Savior, and it reminds us that we are God's chosen way for "getting the word out" concerning Jesus. In a chapter entitled "The Inadequacy of the Non-Christian Religions" Harold Lindsell reminds us that God's primary means of declaring this unique Christ is his people: "God does not reveal himself redemptively through other means than those presently indicated in the Word of God: i.e., through his children's missionary activity in the world."[8]

Why is this emphasis on Jesus as our Savior important? Primarily because our convictions about Jesus Christ as the only way to God and about salvation through the God of the Scriptures alone motivate every Christian for missions, evangelism and outreach. If there are other ways to God, or other "mediators," we have no reason to develop a vision for the world. If there are many ways to God or many ways to obtain salvation, we have no reason to bother with missions at all. (And Jesus would have had no reason to come to earth.) But if Jesus is the only way, we are his ambassadors, pleading with the world to be reconciled to God (see 2 Cor 5).

2. Willing sacrifice: we have a model to imitate. C. T. Studd, a sports star in England in the nineteenth century (who was to English cricket what Michael Jordan is to American basketball), retired from sports so that he could become a pioneer missionary to China, India and Africa. He explained his choice this way: "If Christ be God and gave himself for me, then no sacrifice that I can make for him is too great." Studd caught the idea that Paul communicated to the Philippians in Philippians 2:5-11—that our ultimate goal as Christians is to imitate Jesus by going out as servants, giving ourselves so that others may benefit.

Each summer our church sends fifty to one hundred men and women, young and old, on crosscultural service teams. Every team goes to work and to declare the uniqueness of Jesus Christ through their lives and words. Every team member gives up vacation and pays for the opportunity to go and minister to others. Every summer we get the same amazed question from someone: "Do you mean to tell me that these team members pay to serve?"

"Yes, they do," I reply, "because we believe in following the example of Jesus. He paid for the opportunity to serve us, and we pay for the opportunity to serve others in Jesus' name." In a small way these short-term missionaries understand something of the costs of being an ambassador for Christ:

☐ it costs financially,

☐ it costs in terms of time spent in culture and language learning,

☐ it costs in terms of loss of other opportunities, whether in taking time off without pay or having less vacation time to earn money for schooling.

3. Love: he initiates and we respond. We do not go into the world as witnesses for Christ because we are trying to earn God's favor. We go out of responsive love. We love the Lord our God with all our heart, soul, mind and strength in response to the realization of what he has done for us!

☐ "This is love: not that we loved God, but that he loved us and sent his Son as an atoning sacrifice for our sins" (1 Jn 4:10)

☐ "God demonstrates his own love for us in this: While we were still sinners, Christ died for us" (Rom 5:8)

☐ "We know love by this, that he [Jesus] laid down his life for us—and we ought to lay down our lives for one another" (1 Jn 3:16 NRSV)

Adoniram Judson, the great missionary pioneer to Burma (now Myanmar), illustrated this responsive love when he wrote to his future father-in-law asking for Nancy (also known as Ann) Hazeltine's hand in marriage:

> I have now to ask, whether you can consent to part with your daughter early next Spring, to see her no more in this world; whether you can consent to her departure, and her subjection to the hardships and sufferings of a missionary life; whether you can consent to the dangers of the ocean; to the fatal influence of the southern climate of India; to every kind of want & distress; to degradation, insult, persecution, and perhaps even a violent death.

Two things to note so far: First, Adoniram does not seem to be too skilled in diplomacy as he tries to convince Mr. Hazeltine that he is the right man for Nancy; he definitely does not try to impress his future father-in-law with his ability to care for Nancy. Second, every one of Adoniram's bleak predictions came true for Nancy.

Now Adoniram shifts his appeal. What provides the rationale for the sacrifice? Jesus' love for us.

Can you consent to all this, for the sake of him who left his heavenly throne, and died for her and for you; for the sake of the perishing, immortal souls; for the sake of Zion, and the glory of God? Can you consent to all this, in hope of soon meeting your daughter in the world of glory, with the crown of righteousness, brightened with the acclamations of praise which shall redound to her Savior from the heathens saved, through her means, from eternal woe and despair?[9]

4. *Crosscultural outreach: that everyone may know.* Even if we believe in the uniqueness of Christ, we in the West are often reticent to consider going out into the world to proclaim Jesus because of the damage done by past generations. The gospel's unhealthy link to imperialism and colonialization certainly should motivate us to cultivate greater humility; yet past errors do not relieve the church in any nation from the command to take the gospel to every nation—beginning right at home (our own "Jerusalem"—Acts 1:8). As citizens of the kingdom of Christ, we look for ways to do our part in declaring the unique Christ to the world.

Speaking to this issue as a representative of a country that has been oppressed by colonial rule wrongly blended with Christianity, Ajith Fernando of Sri Lanka separates the errors of the past from the call of the present and the future. Missions endeavors of the past, he notes, "were wrong about Western superiority but not about the supremacy of the Gospel, which incidentally did not originate in the West."[10]

A young woman, an alumna of our youth group, returned from one of the Urbana missionary conventions with a new dedication to crosscultural missions. I asked her whether she had a sense of her destination; she replied boldly and matter-of-factly, "The Muslim world."

"Why?" I asked.

"Because I came to the biblical realization that these Muslims are lost without Jesus Christ." The uniqueness of Christ was sending her out.

Another young woman, deliberating where she would go as a Christian English teacher, watched a video on Mongolia. The interviewer asked a Mongolian man, "What do you think about Jesus Christ?"

The translator interpreted the question, and the Mongolian man replied with a puzzled look, "Jesus Christ—who is this Jesus Christ? I have never heard of this person Jesus Christ."

The man's words sealed that young woman's decision. She determined to go to tell this man and his fellow Mongolians about Jesus Christ so that they could have a chance to respond.

There's That Question Again

Who do you say that Jesus is?

A Hindu man once asked E. Stanley Jones, "What has Christianity to offer that our religion has not?"

He replied, "Jesus Christ."[11]

C. S. Lewis's famous "trilemma" hits us between the eyes with the worldview choice we face. In response to the statement "I can accept Jesus as a great moral teacher but not his claim to be God," Lewis wrote:

> That is one thing we must not say. A man who was merely a man and said the sort of things that Jesus said would not be a great moral teacher. He would either be a lunatic—on the level with the man who says he is a poached egg—or else he would be the Devil of Hell. You must make your choice. Either this man was, and is, the Son of God: or else a madman or something worse. You can shut him up for a fool, you can spit at Him and kill Him as a demon; or you can fall at His feet and call Him Lord and God. But let us not come with any patronizing nonsense about His being a great moral teacher. He has not left that option open to us. He did not intend to.[12]

As we strive to develop a worldview built on biblical teaching, we must contend with certain foundational biblical affirmations:

☐ there is one God (Deut 6:4)

☐ who is the unique Savior (Is 43:11)

☐ who has revealed himself through Jesus (Jn 1:1-14; Heb 1:1-3)

☐ and this Jesus—crucified, resurrected and coming again— is the only way, truth and life; no one comes to God the Father except through him (Jn 14:6; Acts 4:12; 1 Tim 2:5)

If Jesus is the Truth, then our worldview will be enlarged. We cannot rest easy while our friends live apart from the love of Christ. We cannot be content with aspirations to reach our own culture alone.

If Jesus is the unique Savior, we will fully accept God's mandate to do our part so that his glory and gospel are proclaimed to the ends of the earth—whether that means praying, giving, reaching out to internationals in our area or considering crosscultural ministry ourselves.

So who do you really believe Jesus Christ is?

Next Steps

How will you respond personally to this chapter's dangerous question?

1. Explore the Bible for yourself. Examine Jesus' claims to be unique as well as the concept of Jesus as the one-and-only Savior. As you do so, ask yourself, *If this is true, what are the implications for my life, my priorities, my witness and my future?*

2. Ask five friends (including some of other religious faiths), "Who do you say that Jesus is?"

5

• • • • • • •

DO I
BELIEVE
IN HEAVEN?

*Now there is in store for me the
crown of righteousness,
which the Lord, the righteous
Judge, will award to me
on that day.*
(2 Timothy 4:8)

On a one-day, whirlwind tour of Rome, our time in prison stood
out above all other memories and sights. Many believe the
Mamertine Prison to be the place where both Peter and Paul
spent their last days before being executed.

The prison looks like little more than a cave. Twenty or more
prisoners were squeezed into a space not much larger than ten
by twenty feet (three by six meters). A tunnel to an underground
river served both as the exit for human waste and the burial chute
for dead prisoners. The damp, chilly final waiting room for the
condemned was furnished with one oil lamp, filthy water and
inadequate food. The place would have been filled with the
coughing of those afflicted by tuberculosis, the stench of human
decay, the moaning of people in pain, the prayers of dying men.

Although legends and fanciful stories have been associated

with this prison over the centuries (an indentation in the stone wall, for example, has been thought to be an imprint of Peter's face!), it is almost certain that this is the location from which Paul wrote 2 Timothy and, according to F. F. Bruce and others, Philippians.

A firsthand experience of the Mamertine Prison shows these epistles to be all the more miraculous. Under the dim light of that one oil lamp, Paul wrote to Timothy to encourage him to rekindle his spiritual gifts because "God did not give us a spirit of timidity, but a spirit of power, of love and of self-discipline" (2 Tim 1:7). He wrote to Timothy words to inspire endurance:

☐ "Join with me in suffering" (1:8)

☐ "Be strong in the grace that is in Christ Jesus" (2:1)

☐ "God's word is not chained" (2:9)

☐ "Everyone who wants to live a godly life in Christ Jesus will be persecuted" (3:12)

☐ "Preach the Word; be prepared in season and out of season" (4:2)

To the Philippians (from that same prison or a similar setting) Paul wrote words to encourage joy in their respective "prisons":

☐ "What has happened to me has really served to advance the gospel" (1:12)

☐ "Whatever happens, conduct yourselves in a manner worthy of the gospel of Christ" (1:27)

☐ "Your attitude should be the same as that of Christ Jesus" (2:5)

☐ "Rejoice in the Lord" (3:1; 4:4)

☐ "I have learned to be content whatever the circumstances" (4:11)

Time in the Mamertine Prison, combined with a reading of these two letters, led me to the question: how did Paul do it?

How did he maintain his faith, his attitude, his joy and his perseverance in the face of such hardship and suffering?

The answer? Heaven. Paul believed in heaven. His relationship with Jesus Christ and his conviction that he would spend forever with Jesus motivated his endurance. He lived for eternity. As he wrote from that Roman prison, he really believed that "our light and momentary troubles are achieving for us an eternal glory that far outweighs them all" (2 Cor 4:17). He was looking forward to the biblically predicted home where there is unbroken fellowship with God and no more sin and suffering.

Paul's last words—the second letter to Timothy—wrap up his eternal perspective: "Now there is in store for me the crown of righteousness, which the Lord, the righteous Judge, will award to me on that day" (4:8).

To the Philippians he expresses his heavenly focus more frequently:

☐ "For to me, to live is Christ and to die is gain" (Phil 1:21)

☐ "I press on toward the goal to win the prize for which God has called me heavenward in Christ Jesus" (3:14)

☐ "Our citizenship is in heaven" (3:20)

Paul's worldview was built on the reality of the resurrected Christ, and he found motivation and courage in the reality of heaven. His eternal outlook gave him courage to risk, to suffer and even to die.

Every time I think of the Mamertine Prison, I ask myself, *Do I believe in heaven?*

Living as an Existentialist

Any follower of Jesus Christ will emphatically reply, "Yes, I believe in heaven!" So let me ask it another way: is my belief in heaven reflected in the way I plan, the way I make my choices, the priorities I live by?

I find it easy to say that I believe in heaven and yet to live like a functional existentialist, as if this life were all there is. In our materialistic culture it is easy for me to proclaim a hope in heaven but actually put my hope in my career, my achievements or my possessions.

Thinking about my view of heaven, I remember specific times where I or someone else expressed hesitancy to appropriate heaven or live for eternity.

The Gulf War was launched in January 1991. The Middle Eastern location and the involvement of Israel made many evangelicals wonder whether this was the start of Armageddon, the great and final battle to end human history as we know it. A week after the bombing of Baghdad began, my family was heading on a vacation for which we'd been planning and saving for over a year—camping on the Caribbean island of St. John in the U.S. Virgin Islands.

Theologically I should have been hoping for the return of Christ, but humanly I found myself hoping for vacation before the Gulf War brought the "end of the world." I wanted to pray, "Lord, can you delay your return until my vacation is over?" I was thinking with a "this-world" orientation rather than with heaven in mind.

A year later, my wife and I planned to join the Namibian director of Youth for Christ on a drive into the war-torn country of Angola. Two days before we were to depart, four British tourists were machine-gunned to death not far from our destination. I knew that I should have been thinking, *For me to live is Christ and to die is gain,* but in reality I was afraid. Humanly, I wanted safety more than I wanted heaven.

I know I am not alone in failing to integrate my belief in

heaven with my responses to life. My friend Larry, a genuine missionary zealot, told me that he had read about an African city where 25 percent of the males had tested positive for HIV. "You definitely don't want to go there," he said. We asked ourselves how we would respond in the light of heaven, and agreed that a "heaven-bent" response would be "Let's get up right now and go there; these people are knocking at the door of eternity and need an opportunity to respond to Jesus!" But humanly we wanted to run from the thought of disease, suffering and death.

Even dedicated potential missionaries struggle to keep a long-term view of heaven and the eternal. Bernie May, former U.S.A. director of Wycliffe Bible Translators, lists the four major reasons that Wycliffe applicants drop out:

1. They don't want to leave family and friends.

2. Finances—they don't want to raise funds, nor are they willing to live in the insecurity of low income.

3. Concerns for health and safety—for themselves and their families.

4. They don't want to accept the low standard of living they associate with missionary work.[1]

Do you find these reasons shocking? I did. Members of Wycliffe Bible Translators rank among the world's most dedicated missionaries, yet even those who had signed up as WBT career missionaries found it tough to keep eternal perspective when they faced the sacrifices Jesus said would be normative for his disciples.

How Could Heaven Be Better Than This?
A Christian teenager's response helped me identify the problem that we (especially those of us who come from the affluent countries of the world) have in anticipating heaven. When I

n, "Are you looking forward to heaven?" he replied, "I don ι ι.. ow; will there be malls in heaven?"

His answer illustrates the tension in a materialistic society. Having surrounded ourselves with comfort and convenience, we have a hard time believing that heaven will be better than the creature comforts we already enjoy. Why should we long for streets of gold or mansions in heaven when we have shiny malls and luxurious accommodations here and now?

Tony Campolo observes that the materialism of our times has diluted our hunger for the spiritual:

> Ours is an age in which spiritual blessings are being promised to those who buy material things. The spiritual is being absorbed by the physical. The fruit of the spirit, suggests the media, can be had without spiritual disciplines. It is not simply that we are materialists who crave the goods that flood our markets, but that we are now a people who subconsciously have been made to believe that in these things we will find an end to the spiritual longings at the ground of our being.[2]

When "stuff"—material possessions—begins to assuage our spiritual appetites, we start living for this world rather than for eternity. George Hunter identifies secular people (including those of us who call ourselves Christians but are in reality secular in our values) as those who are "looking for life before death"— that is, fulfillment now.[3]

When we are poor, we sing, "This world is not my home; I'm just a-passin' through," but after we become affluent and comfortable, we sing, "This is my Father's world."

The resultant existentialism—living as if this life is all there is—manifests itself in the "deification of life." We run from the reality that we are going to die: we work out to live longer; we undergo operations to make us look younger; we speak and plan as if longevity constituted one of our inalienable rights.

Our inadequate theology of heaven makes us run from hardships. Not only do we fear death, but we also avoid the necessary "dying to self" that comes with following Jesus. We elude sacrifice, run from pain and suffering, and live for the quickest results at the minimum effort.

British evangelist Steve Chalke relates a humorous story about his friend Roy Castle, a Christian leader who was dying of cancer. At the end of a press conference, Roy was feeling terrible, bent over in pain. A reporter sought him out and, after getting Roy's attention, asked, "Roy, how would you feel if you knew you had three months to live?"

He replied slowly, "If I knew that, I'd be the happiest man in this room because I'd be the only one in this room who knows that. The rest of you don't even know if you'll make it to teatime!"[4]

Roy Castle rattled the reporters' perspective because he reminded them that they too faced eternity. And we need such rattling. When we begin to pursue a long and fulfilling life of God's "blessings" (translation: material goods) as our goal, we overlook eternity. God's goal for us may be a life of obedience which is shortened because of the investments we make for eternity, giving up (in Jim Elliot's words) what we cannot keep to gain what we cannot lose. Perhaps the reason some fall away when hardship enters their lives is that they had expected their Christian faith to ensure their escape from problems rather than give an eternal perspective that would strengthen them to endure suffering.

Biblical Realities
The Bible opens our eyes to God's eternal perspective on reality

and reminds us that this world is not our ultimate destination. Eternal life is the goal.

Jesus' prayer for his disciples, the Lord's Prayer, gives a snapshot of the eternal, referring to heaven or the eternal throughout:

Our Father *in heaven,*
hallowed be your name,
your kingdom come,
your will be done
    on earth *as it is in heaven.*
Give us today our daily bread.
Forgive us our debts,
    as we also have forgiven our debtors.
And lead us not into temptation,
but deliver us from the evil one.
For yours is the kingdom and the power and the glory forever.
    Amen. (Mt 6:9-13)

In short, daily bread and forgiveness of sins fit into a life built on eternal perspectives.

No New Testament author wrote about heaven more than Paul—and he lived out his convictions. He consistently risked his security in preaching the gospel because he saw his citizenship as being in heaven (Phil 3:20). He taught that the sufferings of this life are nothing compared to the glory of heaven (2 Cor 4:17). His mission endeavors were motivated by heaven, and he went out in ready obedience to the Lord of heaven, Jesus Christ. Facing persecutions in Jerusalem, he told the Ephesian elders, "I only know that in every city the Holy Spirit warns me that prison and hardships are facing me. However, I consider my life worth nothing to me, if only I may finish the race and complete the task the Lord Jesus has given me—the task of testifying to the gospel of God's grace" (Acts 20:23-24).

Writing to the Romans, Paul established his sense of priorities based on his heavenly destination: "For none of us lives to himself alone and none of us dies to himself alone. If we live, we live to the Lord; and if we die, we die to the Lord. So, whether we live or die, we belong to the Lord" (Rom 14:7-8).

Why? According to Galatians 2:20, "I have been crucified with Christ and I no longer live, but Christ lives in me. The life I live in the body, I live by faith in the Son of God, who loved me and gave himself for me."

And Paul exhorts us all to follow his example: "Set your minds on things above, not on earthly things. For you died, and your life is now hidden with Christ in God" (Col 3:2-3).

In contrast to our attempts to run from death and to deny its reality, Paul lived with eternity in mind, and he made his decisions accordingly.

Heaven in Missions History

The women and men of missions history have followed this heavenly motivation. The first European missionaries to Africa believed in heaven. When they packed for their mission, legend tells us, they carried their worldly possessions in coffins, because a coffin was seen as essential equipment. They expected that once they left their temporal homes they would never return.

Legends like this are told about missionary pioneers like George Grenfell and Alexander MacKay. Grenfell's first wife died after only one year in Africa. He later remarried, and four of the children of this marriage succumbed to the diseases and fevers of Africa. He opened work on the Congo River, where three of the first four missionaries died in the first year of service. The work of his mission station led to many conversions, but they came at a great sacrifice.

MacKay's story has a similar ring. Called to pioneer work in Uganda, he accurately predicted that some of his initial team of eight would die. After the first year, five had died; after the second, MacKay was the only one left. MacKay was instrumental in bringing the gospel to the Baganda people of Uganda, but this ministry cost him dearly: sickness, deaths of other coworkers, violent attempts on his life, and his eventual death at age forty of malaria.

Some estimate that as many as 60 percent of the pioneer missionaries to Africa died within the first two years of ministry. So why would they go? They believed that Jesus Christ should be proclaimed, and they believed in heaven!

And the same is true today. At the Lausanne II Conference in Manila in the late 1980s, George Otis remarked in passing, "Perhaps we have had little success in reaching the Muslim world because we've had too few who are willing to be martyrs." He urged the contemporary church of Jesus Christ to rekindle our zeal for heaven rather than continuing our quest for safety.

In a September 1995 speech to the U.S. secretary of state's Open Forum, Bob Seiple, president of World Vision-USA, referred to losing twenty-two World Vision colleagues in the past eight years. All of them were killed in their pursuit of showing mercy and bringing about justice for the sake of the eternal kingdom.[5]

The issue was brought home to our church not long ago, when we got word that the seven-year-old daughter of one of our missionary families had died of complications related to cerebral malaria. This family was in a remote part of northern Mozambique, where appropriate medical care had not been available, at least not in time to save the child.

Many of our home-church supporters thought that the girl's death was a tragic mistake. "Maybe they never should have been there in the first place." "Do you think they should go back with their other two children?"

The child's father, Stuart, offered a different perspective. In the midst of his great grief and anguish, he told us how four Mozambican pastors—all of whom had left places of greater comfort to come with Stuart to serve in this out-of-the-way region—provided deep consolation. "As we stood by my daughter's grave, I realized that all four of these men had buried at least one of their own children for the sake of the advance of the gospel."

Temporal sacrifices because we believe in heaven. For many, the sacrifice involves not death but loneliness, singleness, sickness, poverty, hardship. Still, we sacrifice because we are ready to live out our convictions that eternity is real and this world is not our final destination.

Implications for Our Worldview

What happens when people really believe in heaven?

A vision of heaven gives us strength to endure hardship. The writer of Hebrews encouraged his readers to stay faithful by reviewing the great "Hall of Fame" of faith (Heb 11). Concluding with the example of Jesus, he urges his readers to "run with perseverance the race marked out for us" by keeping their eyes fixed on Jesus. Then he points to Jesus' eternal vision: "Jesus . . . who *for the joy set before him* endured the cross" (12:1-2).

A missionary mother in Eastern Europe, experiencing a way of life she would never have chosen for herself, reflected this eternal perspective when she said, "I'm not a foreigner because I chose Romania; I'm a foreigner because I chose Jesus."

Keeping her eyes on Jesus and the eternal prize motivates her to persevere.

Philip Yancey summarized the motivational power of the eternal in a *Christianity Today* column:

For years, all the New Testament talk about eternal rewards embarrassed me. Now, however, I see eternal rewards as the ultimate form of delayed gratification.

Why do missionary relief workers volunteer for hellish places like Somalia, Rwanda, and the Sudan? I have interviewed these workers, and among other motives they mention the prospect of reward. They hope to hear someday, "Well done, thou good and faithful servant."[6]

A vision of heaven gives us motivation for great and sacrificial courage. The great pioneer against racism in the United States, Martin Luther King Jr., said, "No one really knows why they're alive until they know what they'd die for." We need a vision for our life that supersedes our desires for self-preservation.

Bob Seiple, in his speech to the secretary of state's Open Forum, recounted an extended conversation with Lady Veronica, wife of Fitzroy MacLean, whose exploits in World War II became the inspiration for Secret Agent 007, James Bond. Lady Veronica critiqued the modern era by observing, "I've always been surrounded by men of courage. The problem today is that too many people are afraid of death."[7]

If the fear of death paralyzes us, we will never venture into the poor places, the violent places and the dangerous places of the world—the places that are most lacking in the knowledge of the good news of Jesus Christ. Without risk-takers with eternity in their hearts, who will reach the gangs of the cities, the impoverished, those dying of AIDS, the terrorists?

A youth group from our church prepared for mission in

Burkina Faso, West Africa. The parents raised a number of health concerns—especially about HIV/AIDS. We did our best to satisfy their concerns, but one mother simply would not rest. She bombarded us with questions that were, in effect, smoke screens for her fears. Finally the woman's sixteen-year-old daughter burst out, "Mom, if I go to Burkina Faso and die there, I guess I'll just see you in heaven!" She was exhorting her mother to adopt an eternal perspective.

When Jesus challenged his disciples in Luke 9:23—"If anyone would come after me, he must deny himself and take up his cross daily and follow me"—he was calling them to be courageous, sacrificial and bold. He was calling them to die to themselves.

Involvement in the global enterprise of following Christ always requires death in various shapes and sizes. Some will literally be asked to die (Jn 12:24), while others will be asked to die to selfishness, materialism, consumerism and all the other enemies of the Jesus-exalting gospel. Dietrich Bonhoeffer's most famous statement—"When Jesus calls a man, he bids him come and die"—urges us to take courage for the sake of Christ's kingdom.

What's the rationale? "I've got a mansion just over the hilltop": I'm investing in eternity.

A vision of heaven helps detach us from our "stuff." In *Give Up Your Small Ambitions* Michael Griffiths bluntly addresses those contemplating crosscultural ministry: "You will need to accept the fact of being poor."[8]

As I read this, I immediately thought, *Why would I willingly choose to be poor?* Then I remembered Paul's words in 2 Corinthians 8:9: "For you know the grace of our Lord Jesus Christ, that though he was rich, yet for your sakes he became poor, so that you through his poverty might become rich."

When Paul reminded the Philippians of Jesus' sacrifice, he appealed to an expectation of heaven:

☐ imitate Jesus (Phil 2:5),

☐ who let go of his heavenly rights (v. 6)

☐ and became not only a human, but a servant (v. 7),

☐ and not just a servant, but a crucified servant (v. 8);

☐ remember too God's ultimate exaltation of Jesus (vv. 9-11),

so that you too can persevere.

Writing to Timothy about those who are rich in this present world (which includes almost all of us in Western society), Paul encouraged them (and us!)

not to be arrogant nor to put their hope in wealth, which is so uncertain, but to put their hope in God, who richly provides us with everything for our enjoyment. Command them to do good, to be rich in good deeds, and to be generous and willing to share. In this way they will lay up treasure for themselves as a firm foundation for the coming age, so that they may take hold of the life that is truly life. (1 Tim 6:17-19)

If auditors look to evaluate someone's "net worth" statement, they can see in financial terms what the investor really believes in. Examining the assets, they may conclude, "This person really believes in real estate," or "This person really believes in mutual funds."

If an auditor looked at your checkbook, your tax returns or the way you use your most precious resource—time—could he or she conclude, "This person really believes in heaven"? That was Paul's challenge to the people in Timothy's church, and that's the challenge for us. Are we living with a spirit of detachment from our stuff because we know that all our resources are given to us by God to be invested for eternity?

Living It Out

The other day we sang an old hymn that reminded me of Paul in the Mamertine Prison in Rome. The chorus goes, "Faith of our fathers, holy faith; we will be true to thee till death." One of the verses speaks of the children of martyrs: "How sweet would be their children's fate, if they, like them, could die for Thee." What a radical song! I had to think twice before I committed myself to sing it. Did I really want to act that strongly on my belief in heaven?

Our lived-out belief in heaven changes our worldview because it suddenly awakens us to the fact that life is more than this world and all that we can accumulate. Convictions of the reality of heaven inspire generosity, encourage perseverance in the face of opposition and give us the joy that Paul had—even in prison.

Do you believe in heaven?

Next Steps

1. Think through three or four decisions that you are facing over the next six months, and ask, "How do I face these decisions differently if I *really* believe in heaven?"

2. Go to a cemetery and read the headstones to see what people thought was really important about their lives. Then take some time to think and pray through your own sense of life direction and purpose.

6
• • • • • • •

Dangerous Question #3

DO I
BELIEVE
IN HELL?

Then they will go away to eternal punishment, but the righteous to eternal life.
(Matthew 25:46)

Over twenty years ago psychiatrist Karl Menninger wrote a book entitled *Whatever Became of Sin?* Perhaps we need a sequel to that book: *Whatever Became of Hell?*

Although discussing topics like the spirit world and the reality of Satan and his angels is acceptable in many Christian circles today, we seldom hear much about judgment, hell, eternal damnation or the concept of everlasting suffering for those who have not trusted Jesus.

Ajith Fernando of Sri Lanka has written *Crucial Questions About Hell* in an attempt to address this oversight. He shows how Jesus spoke and taught more about hell than about heaven, yet few of us give much study or thought to the subject. Fernando observes, "If one generation neglects the doctrine of hell, the next generation will reject it."[1]

A Personal Testimony

I do not write about hell from a relaxed or casual attitude. The horrible idea of eternal judgment strikes me deeply, and a recent conversation drove the reality of hell even further into my heart.

My wife and I sat down several months ago in a restaurant with a relative, a man almost eighty years old. In previous conversations we had articulated the gospel, but he had given little response. This night we sensed that the conversation needed to go in a different direction. Rather than focusing on the good news that Jesus has purchased eternal life for us and now offers it as a gift, we took the discussion in the direction of warning. We talked about the justice and holiness of God and the reality of hell.

The conversation got intense at times, escalating almost to the point of argument, but the man would not budge from his position. He believed that God has no right to condemn anyone to hell. We explained that people choose hell by virtue of their disobedience and their rejection of God's love through Jesus Christ. He wanted to discuss the fate of the "heathen," those in remote areas or foreign lands who have had no opportunity to respond to Christ. We tried to keep the conversation focused on him, since he obviously did have a choice to make about Jesus Christ.

The dialogue volleyed back and forth for ninety minutes or more, until the man brought everything to a screeching halt with this exclamation: "If there is a God who allows people to go to hell, I would never want to spend eternity with him. I choose hell."

I knew from his reply that he misunderstood the love of God, that he could not grasp the mystery of God's holiness, justice and mercy working together, that he took eternity far too lightly.

But at that moment I wanted to throw away my belief system. I thought about rationalizing away all the biblical texts concerning God's judgment. The personal realization of a loved one's choice of hell can wreak havoc on one's theological system and worldview.

Peter Cotterell addressed the interplay of subjective experience with the doctrine of hell when he wrote, "The Christian may be supposed to believe in hell but concern for unconverted relatives may mean a rejection of that particular doctrine."[2] The emotional blow of our relative's making such a choice forced me back to the Scriptures. What do I really believe about hell?

A Theologian's Perspective

An article by Norman Geisler proved helpful as I explored the question: "Everything You Wanted to Know About Hell but Were Afraid to Ask."[3] Geisler identifies the core biblical teachings on hell, highlighting seven statements which I summarize here.

1. Jesus taught the existence of hell. Jesus warned about "the One who can destroy both soul and body in hell" (Mt 10:28). He told a story of a rich man in hell (Lk 16:19-31), advised temporary sacrifices in this life in order to avoid the destination of "hell, where the fire never goes out" (Mk 9:43-44), and predicted that those who had not acted in mercy would be cursed and assigned to "the eternal fire prepared for the devil and his angels" (Mt 25:41).

2. The Bible teaches that there is a hell. To affirm the range of biblical teaching on hell and judgment, Geisler quotes from Hebrews, 2 Thessalonians and finally Revelation 20:13-15: "Death and Hades gave up the dead that were in them, and each person was judged according to what he had done. Then death and Hades were thrown into the lake of fire. The lake of fire is the second death. If anyone's name was not found written in the book of life, he was thrown into the lake of fire."

3. God's love demands a hell. Geisler's article points out the fallacy of the argument that a loving God could not send a person to hell and explains rather that "a God of love cannot force people to love Him." God does not coerce. Geisler concludes, "Those who do not wish to love God must be allowed not to love Him. Those who do not wish to be with Him must be allowed to be separated from Him. Hell is this eternal separation from God." In a sense my eighty-year-old relative could make his choice because God loved him enough to give him freedom.

4. Human dignity demands a hell. Following on his love, God gives us free choice. God respects our dignity and refuses to force us into a relationship with him against our will.

5. God's justice demands a hell. The psalmist observes that the wicked sometimes prosper in this life but God, in his justice, brings the wicked to condemnation: "Then I understood their final destiny" (Ps 73:17). Ultimate judgment comes because God's holiness requires that sin be punished.

6. God's sovereignty demands a hell. "Unless there is a hell, there is no final victory over evil," Geisler argues. If God is sovereign, there must be a final triumph over evil. The condemnation of Satan and the wicked to hell is that ultimate conquest of sin.

7. The cross of Christ implies hell. Finally Geisler asks, "Why the Cross unless there is a hell? If there is no hell to shun, then the Cross is a sham. Christ's death is robbed of its eternal significance unless there is an eternal separation from God from which people need to be delivered."

What Do We Believe About Hell?

Geisler articulates well an overview of some of the biblical teaching on hell, but we still need to make it personal. The question "Do I believe in hell?" is not truly dangerous until we wrestle with its meaning and the implications for our lives.

Engaging the subject of hell contradicts the judgmentless spirit of our age. In our day no one wants to suffer the consequences of wrongdoing. We find legal loopholes to escape the consequences of breaking the law. We want to attribute our bad behavior to our dysfunctional family, so that we ourselves are not held responsible. We want God to be merciful to us no matter how we respond to him. Geisler writes, "In this pluralistic age, [hell] seems too harsh a punishment just for believing the wrong thing."[4]

The doctrine of hell forces us to deal with other tough questions.

1. What do we believe about judgment? Throughout the biblical accounts a principle of judgment appears, a principle that stands in total contrast to the "I am a victim and therefore I am not to be held responsible" attitude promoted in our culture.

Fernando cites A. W. Tozer's observation that "the vague and tenuous hope that God is too kind to punish the ungodly has become a deadly opiate to the consciences of millions." Fernando then goes on, "When they come under conviction and think that they should take the costly step of repentance, something inside them says, 'Don't worry, it's not going to be that bad.' "[5] We convince ourselves that God's mercy exists but his judgment and holiness do not.

We say that we should not be held responsible for our sins; the Bible says that "the soul who sins is the one who will die" (Ezek 18:4) and that "the wages of sin is death" (Rom 6:23). We want God to meet us on our terms; the Bible says that if we do not meet God on his terms, the result is a chasm between us and God so that he does not even hear our prayers (Ps 66:18; Is 59:2).

We hope that everyone will receive eternal life, and we quote John 3:16: "For God so loved the world that he gave his one and only Son, that whoever believes in him shall not perish but have everlasting life." But somehow we manage to overlook John 3:18: "Whoever believes in him is not condemned, but whoever does not believe stands condemned already because he has not believed in the name of God's one and only Son." If we get as far as John 3:36—"Whoever believes in the Son has eternal life, but whoever rejects the Son will not see life, for God's wrath remains on him"—we begin to get the picture: our choices have eternal consequences. This we call judgment.

The Bible asserts that "man is destined to die once, and after that to face judgment" (Heb 9:27). No reincarnations into a better life, no second chances. We live out our fifty or sixty or seventy years, and then we stand before God responsible for the life we lived and the choices we made. In biblical language, whatever we have sown we will reap (Gal 6:9-10).

2. *What do we believe about the fate of those who never hear the gospel?* As my wife and I talked with my relative about hell and judgment, he tried to deflect the issue away from himself by raising the question of the eternal destiny of those who have no knowledge of Jesus Christ. We steered the conversation back to him, but his question was and is valid. Does someone who has never known about the saving gift of forgiveness in Christ stand automatically condemned before God?

Every responder to this problem ultimately defers to God's mercy and justice. We cannot offer the final answer; only God can. But we should always keep in mind the conclusion stated earlier in the discussion of Dangerous Question 1, "Who is Jesus?": if there is another way of salvation outside of Jesus Christ, God has not told us what it is.

In dealing with this tough question, we must act on what God has revealed in the Scriptures. First, it seems that those who preceded Christ and were saved "by faith" believed that God would cover their sins through a Savior. They received salvation because they anticipated God's intervention on their behalf "from a distance" (Heb 11:13). Thus we can see how Old Testament saints received eternal life.

In modern times the parallel would be people who, by virtue of God's grace, conclude that they cannot save themselves and that God will provide a Savior. They put their trust in this unnamed Savior, and when a Christian witness or missionary comes and names this Savior as Jesus, the people readily turn to faith in him.

Stories of such encounters, although exceptional in missions history, provide wonderful testimony of God's work to prepare people by his sovereign grace. Both Don Richardson's *Eternity in Their Hearts* and Paul Eshlemann's *I Just Saw Jesus* illustrate such God-initiated actions in recent missions history. They relate stories of ethnic groups in remote locations who had been prepared by God to hear the gospel, even to the point of having local legends about God's Son who was sent to redeem the world. When Christians came with the gospel message, huge numbers of these people responded immediately.

A second response to this question usually examines the issue of "living up to the light that has been revealed." When this question arose in apologetic discussions in my student years at the University of Massachusetts, I appealed to Romans 1:18 and the concept of "general revelation." Here the idea is simply that people will be judged according to the light revealed to them. Therefore, so the argument goes, a person with no knowledge of Jesus Christ will be judged based on his or her ability to live according to an internal moral compass or the spiritual knowledge possessed.

The flaw with this argument is that it implies that "living up to the light that has been revealed" is possible. Romans 1:18-20 says that everyone has some knowledge of God and therefore they are without excuse. Yet Romans 1:21 and the following chapters 2—4 remind us that *no one lives up to the light revealed to them.* People choose to be disobedient to that light; therefore God acts justly and punishes their sins. If people could and did live up to the light that has been revealed to them, why would a Savior need to come?

The third response to this question brings us face to face with God's choice to grant his people responsibility to bring the message of his love to those who have had no opportunity to respond. From this response comes the missionary commitment to bring the gospel across cultures, "to preach the gospel where Christ was not known" (Rom 15:20).

Paul addresses the fate of those who have never heard in Romans 10:

"Everyone who calls on the name of the Lord will be saved." How, then, can they call on the one they have not believed in? And how can they believe in the one of whom they have not heard? And how can they hear without someone preaching to them? And how can they preach unless they are sent? As it is written, "How beautiful are the feet of those who bring good news!" (vv. 13-15)

Since there is salvation in no one other than Jesus and there is no other name under heaven by which people can be saved, we must assume that people without Christ are lost. To remedy this, we must send out those who will preach the good news of Jesus.

3. What do I believe about annihilation (or conditional mortality)? Two views on hell compete with each other in the camp of those who call themselves biblical Christians. The traditional view states that after judgment the saved go on to eternal life with Jesus while the lost go to eternal hell with the devil and his angels to suffer eternal punishment apart from God. Those adhering to the doctrine of annihilation believe, however, that the saved go on to eternal life with Jesus while the lost go to the fires of hell where they are consumed and cease to be.

Various books debate this issue, among them Ajith Fernando's *Crucial Questions About Hell,* John Wenham's *The Goodness of God* (InterVarsity Press, 1986), Robert Peterson's *Hell on Trial* (Presbyterian & Reformed, 1995) and Edward Fudge's *The Fire That Consumes* (Providential Press, 1982). We face four possible positions:

a. Jesus' death saves everyone from hell, whether they believe in him or not. While this position, universalism, holds great romantic and emotional appeal, it finds little biblical support.

b. People without Christ go to hell and suffer until they change their minds and decide for Christ. Origen proposed this view in the third century, thinking hell to be a place where the unrighteous are disciplined until they eventually repent and receive salvation. The result of this position was functionally universalism again, and it gave birth to some of the ideas associated with purgatory. Origen's view represents an interesting attempt to merge the justice of God with the desire for universal salvation, but it too has little biblical support.

c. People without Christ are judged and then consumed—that is, they cease to be. The annihilationist position seeks to integrate the biblical teaching with human revulsion at the thought of an eternity of suffering for sins in a finite lifetime. This view might also be called conditional immortality, the notion that God promises immortality only to those who find salvation in Christ. Those adhering to the annihilationist position focus on God's judgment as punish*ment* (a one-time, final administration of justice) versus punish*ing* (an ongoing state of suffering for sin). Many key evangelical leaders, including Clark Pinnock, F. F. Bruce and John Stott, have advocated (or encouraged serious consideration of) this view.

There are two major problems with the annihilationist position. One is objective: the Scripture passages that place eternal life in juxtaposition to eternal death, thereby making them parallels (see *d,* below). The second is subjective: the annihilationist position dulls our sense of the significance of hell. If we die without Christ and then simply cease to exist, what is the judgment? Being extinguished or consumed seems far less severe than suffering for eternity.

A friend who describes himself as "actively pagan" remarked after I explained the annihilationist position, "That's what I believe already: live a wild life, party till you die, and then nothing—you cease to be."

d. People without Christ are judged and sentenced to a Christless eternity where (in a parallel eternity to heaven) they suffer forever. This position paints by far the harshest picture. In reaction to this view, David Edwards identified God as the "eternal torturer."[6]

But harshest or not, is it biblical? Matthew 25:41 refers to people being thrown into "the eternal fire prepared for the devil and his angels." In that same passage the eternal destination of the saved and that of the damned seem parallel: "Then they will go away to eternal punishment, but the righteous to eternal life" (v. 46).

Jesus' reference to eternal punishment in Mark 9:48—"where 'their worm does not die, and the fire is not quenched' "—seems to suggest an endless state, and the picture of the condemned rich man in Luke 16:19-31 certainly implies that he is living with a conscious awareness of suffering in hell's torment.

To the Thessalonians, Paul wrote about those who would suffer everlasting destruction as part of their punishment for not knowing and obeying Jesus Christ (2 Thess 1:7-9). Revelation 20:10 paints the cruelest picture of all, referring to the wicked being thrown into the "lake of burning sulfur," where they will be "tormented day and night for ever and ever."

Cotterell summarizes the awfulness of hell as viewed from this traditional stance: "The real horror of the concept of hell is that of its endlessness."[7] He then goes on to urge caution in the way we deal with the biblical pictures: "That the doctrine of an eternal hell is there in Scripture is beyond dispute. That the imagery is just that, imagery, is similarly beyond dispute. What it is that corresponds to that imagery we simply do not know."[8]

Whether we advocate position c or d regarding hell (positions a and b require that we disregard the Bible), the message of the Scriptures concerning hell is severe: people bound for hell forfeit eternal life with Jesus Christ. Their disregard for (or lack of knowledge of) the gospel eliminates for them the possibility of heaven and the endless pleasures promised to those who know Christ. Either view of hell should compel us to encourage people to repent and turn to Jesus.

4. What do I believe about the spiritual world? Any discussion about hell inevitably raises questions about the devil and his angels, the beings we call demons. A full study of these evil counterparts to God's angels requires another book or more, but several important issues need to be taken into consideration as we examine our worldview.

Here again the Bible must establish the basis for our convictions. In conversations with fellow Christians I find that many beliefs about demons, spiritual warfare, territorial spirits or Satan are based on anecdotal experiences (their own or somebody else's) or from the pages of *This Present Darkness* or another Frank Peretti novel. The notion of the "levels" of hell, for example, comes not from biblical teaching but from Dante's *Divine Comedy.* Whatever we believe about the spiritual world, the demonic or the angelic should find its basis in the Bible.

Building on the biblical teaching about the spiritual world, we recognize that the principal role of Satan and his angels is to blind people to the gospel of life through Jesus Christ: "The god of this age has blinded the minds of unbelievers, so that they cannot see the light of the gospel of the glory of Christ, who is the image of God" (2 Cor 4:4).

Satan, who disguises himself as an angel of light (2 Cor 11:14), needs to be opposed through spiritual battle, which includes prayer, faith, truth, the gospel message and the "sword of the Spirit, which is the word of God" (see Eph 6:10-18). Only as we engage in that battle can we help to turn people from darkness to light, from the power of Satan to the power of God (Acts 26:18).

Ephesians 6 reminds us that we live in a spiritual world. In *Christianity with Power* Charles Kraft points out that many Western Christians function with a materialistic or rationalistic worldview. In reaction to extreme practices of blaming the devil or his demons for every hardship and every temptation, many of us confine our beliefs about the spiritual world to our faith in

God and our hope of eternal life. We assume that weather systems result from natural forces unrelated to the spiritual. We treat mental illness with psychological therapy and drugs. If we are physically ill, we go to the doctor. Given our reductionistic view, we seldom ask questions like "Is an evil spirit the cause of this affliction?" Kraft does not intend for us to be looking for demons under every rock; he merely wants to call us into a biblical view of the world, an understanding that spiritual forces are in conflict, striving with eternal consequences: "For our struggle is not against flesh and blood, but against the rulers, against the authorities, against the powers of this dark world and against the spiritual forces of evil in the heavenly realms" (Eph 6:12).

Finally, our beliefs must take into account the ultimate victory of God. In describing the phenomena of spiritual warfare, some paint a picture that is clearly dualistic: God (good) and Satan (evil) are presented as if they were on some equal footing in the battle. This contradicts the biblical accounts, which clearly show that God, as sovereign Lord and Creator, will win the final battle (see Rev 12:9; 20:2, 7). Satan, a fallen angel, and his demons (also fallen angels) operate with limited power, even to the point where they must ask God's permission to act (Job 1:6-12). The demons tremble at the appearance of Jesus in the New Testament, and the work of Jesus Christ—his death and resurrection—confirms the ultimate victory, "so that by his death he might destroy him who holds the power of death—that is, the devil" (Heb 2:14). We can affirm with confidence that greater is Jesus, who is in us, than Satan, the lord of this world (1 Jn 4:4).

If Hell Is a Reality . . .

How will our lives change if we take the biblical doctrine of hell seriously?

Ajith Fernando presents telling examples of how an understanding of people's lostness without Christ motivated some of the great heroes of Christian history:

The seventeenth century preacher, Samuel Rutherford, once told a person, "I would lay my dearest joys in the gap between you and eternal destruction." Hudson Taylor said, "I would have never thought of going to China had I not believed that the Chinese were lost and needed Christ." D. L. Moody told an audience in London, "If I believed there was no hell, I am sure I would be off tomorrow for America." He said he would gladly give up going from town to town spending day and night "urging men to escape the damnation of hell." William Booth said he would wish that his Salvation Army workers might spend "one night in hell" in order to see the urgency of their evangelistic task.[9]

A vision of hell and a seriousness about impending judgment obviously motivated some of the great leaders in church history. What impact will it have on us?

A message that includes warning. After Jim heard that I had converted to Jesus Christ, he took it upon himself to become my verbal persecutor. Whenever he was in my presence, he would intensify his use of Jesus' name as profanity. I tried to laugh it off, because Jim was the local tough guy and no one dared to mess with him.

After about three weeks of this mocking of Jesus, I prayed for courage and then confronted Jim with a warning: "Whether you respect my beliefs is irrelevant, Jim, but this one thing you should know: you will be held accountable before God for every empty word that you speak. If you choose to take Jesus' name in vain, that's your prerogative, but bear in mind that 'men will have to give account on the day of judgment for every careless word they have spoken. For by your words you will be acquitted, and by your words you will be condemned' " (Mt 12:36-37).

Jim stood there stunned. I expected him to punch my face in, but he just said "OK" and walked away.

I had confronted Jim with the reality of judgment, of the prospect of being held responsible before God for his actions and choices. Later that year Jim wrote to me, "Thanks for being one of the only people who ever cared about me." My warning had communicated to him that I did not want to see him standing judgment.

The short and difficult-to-understand book of Jude contains this unusual command: "Be merciful to those who doubt; snatch others from the fire and save them; to others show mercy, mixed with fear" (22-23). Mercy mixed with fear. Good news mixed with warnings. Snatch people out of the fires of hell by warning them.

If God's loving invitation to eternal life does not motivate us to share the good news with people, what about the bad news? What about warning people to flee from the wrath to come? We would do well to soberly confront people with the reality (in C. S. Lewis's terms) that they can choose to follow Jesus and say, "Thy will be done," or they can choose to reject Jesus, who as the Judge will say to them, "Thy will be done," releasing them to their destination of choice, the fires of hell.

Increased urgency. The pioneer who opened the interiors of China to the gospel, Hudson Taylor, thought often about the reality of hell, and this fueled his zeal to preach the gospel to those who had never heard it before. His nightmares of thousands of Chinese plunging over a cliff into a Christless eternity urged him on.

When Taylor returned to his own country, England, and

became aware of the relative complacency of the Christian church in a land where the gospel remained accessible to all, he was appalled. He interpreted his compatriots' nonchalance about the preaching of the gospel to those who had never heard about Jesus as disregard for the doctrines of hell and judgment.

Increased compassion and prayer. If we love people, our hearts will be broken over their lostness and impending judgment. Compassion changes the way we look at and pray for the lost materialist, the renegade racist, the abortion-clinic doctor, the promiscuous hetero- or homosexual. Concluding that hell is a reality does not give us license to condemn, scorn or fear those who are unsaved.

Paul illustrates this compassionate passion in Romans 9 when he refers to the lostness of his fellow Jews as a source of "great sorrow and unceasing anguish"; he even wished that he could sacrifice his own salvation for their sakes (vv. 1-3).

Charles Finney and D. L. Moody drew crowds by the thousands to hear their impassioned pleas to be reconciled to God and escape the judgment of hell. A. B. Simpson, the founder of the Christian and Missionary Alliance, built a worldwide ministry based on tearful prayers for those in the world who had no knowledge of Jesus Christ.

John Stott reflects this brokenness and deep compassion when he rebukes a casual attitude about hell: "I repudiate with all the vehemence of which I am capable the glibness, what almost appears to be glee, with which the Evangelicals speak about hell."[10]

The doctrine of hell is not given to us so that we can write people off and treat their eternal destiny lightly. If anything, we should be moved to tears as we contemplate the destiny of people without a Savior.

Targeting those with no opportunity. If we believe in hell, then we feel great remorse when we hear of people who have no opportunity to hear the good news about Jesus. Oswald J. Smith of Toronto's People's Church used to say, "No one should hear the gospel twice before everyone has heard it once." He was burdened for those who had never heard, reflecting Paul's desire to preach "where Christ was not known" (Rom 15:20).

In spite of the wonderful advances of the Christian church around the world, experts still estimate that between two and three billion people have no opportunity to hear the gospel and respond. The doctrine of hell ought to burden us deeply to mobilize the church to get the good news to these people.

The Impact of Hell

How does hell influence our worldview? If we ignore the biblical teaching about the eternal fate of those outside of Christ, we can live quietly, complacently, surrounded with nice people whom we never ruffle with discussions about judgment or the penalty of sin. But if hell is a reality, and we let awareness of that reality sink in to the way we look at the world, we will be compelled to speak out about Jesus Christ. Our proclamation of the gospel will include warning as well as good news. Our prayers will expand to include not only unsaved friends and relatives but also people and groups around the world who have no knowledge of Jesus Christ.

Like Jonathan Edwards or Hudson Taylor, we will be prompted to action by our vision of lost people headed toward a Christless eternity.

Next Steps

1. Take a half-day away from your normal routine to pray

through a list of friends and relatives who do not yet know Jesus Christ. Pray that God will, by the work of his Holy Spirit, convict them of sin, of righteousness and of judgment (according to Jn 16:8-11).

2. Initiate a discussion on the topic of judgment with a friend who has not embraced the Christian faith. Ask that person, "If there is a hell, would you want to be warned?"

7
● ● ● ● ● ● ●

Dangerous Question #4

DOES CHRISTIANITY MATTER?

*... Men of Issachar, who
understood the times and knew
what Israel should do.*
(1 Chronicles 12:32)

Three demons were having a conversation about how to distract
the church of Jesus Christ from its appointed mission to the
world. The first demon said, "Let's tell them that there is no
heaven; then they will lose their motivation because they have
no reward ahead."

"No," said the second, "I have a better idea. Let's tell them
that there's no hell. If there's no threat of judgment and condemnation, why should they bother proclaiming their good news?"

Demon number three, the oldest and wisest of the group,
replied, "No, I know the best plan. Tell the church that there's
no reason. Tell them that their faith is primarily for their personal

enrichment and betterment. Make them think that Christian faith should not get stained by involvement in a sinful world and should be kept separated from it. If we can get them to believe this, it won't matter if they believe in heaven and hell, because they'll see their faith as relevant only to them."

This fictional demon dialogue illustrates what has happened to the worldview of many Christians. We have become convinced that the mission of the church is to make sure that Christians are happy and content. We focus on our own fellowship and doctrinal purity, often at the expense of interaction with the world. As a result we render the church virtually irrelevant to the issues in our world.

And the world notices. John Stott once recounted a conversation he'd had with two agnostics, university students with whom he was talking after an evangelistic presentation. As he explained the historical veracity of the resurrection of Jesus Christ, one of the students shot back, "But whether Jesus rose from the dead or not is not the issue. The issue is that Christianity is irrelevant to our world."

That student hit a nerve that should awaken us all. Am I really convinced that the truths I believe matter in the world today? Does my faith apply to the campus, the marketplace, the neighborhood? Am I living as if my Christianity were a private concern that has little bearing on my day-to-day existence? Or am I willing to wrestle with what faith means in contemporary society as we approach the year 2000?

Contemporary Realities

The unfortunate development of "privatized religion," in which my faith affects my frame of mind, my emotional state, but has little integration with daily living, has exaggerated this disconnectedness of faith and life.

Reflecting on the European situation, Peter Cotterell illustrates the decline of Christian faith over the twentieth century because the church failed to adequately address the world wars: "There was a widespread abandoning of religion after the First World War and continuing through and beyond the Second, and it was abandoned because it was seen as being irrelevant and unbelievable."[1] Western European Christianity still suffers the repercussions of this perceived irrelevance.

Privatized faith implies that our personal beliefs about God reflect only our vertical relationship to him and not our relationship with the human race around us. Stephen Neill, the great missionary statesman, points out in *Crises of Belief* that in one university context 60.4 percent professed a belief in God and nearly 40 percent stated that they had a fairly regular prayer life. Students saw a need for God to complete their worldview and to ameliorate the apparent meaninglessness of life, but they saw no need for organized religion. The corporate body of believers acting through churches or societies was regarded as unimportant.[2]

A church leader relayed his dismay that in the months that followed October 1989 and the beginnings of the dissolution of the Soviet empire, he never heard any Christian perspective on these great and tumultuous changes in his church. He described his church situation this way:

Our pastor went through these five months or more without one reference to or prayer for what was happening in Eastern Europe. We were hearing it every night on the news, and even secular broadcasters were discussing the role of the Christian church in these changes. But at church? Not a word. The message that got communicated to me and my family was that Christian faith is a personal thing that has nothing to do with the changing world around us.

His comments made me think of the humorous way that the potential irrelevance of pastors was once described: a minister is "six days invisible, one day incomprehensible."

Related to privatized religion is a phenomenon identified by George Hunter as "mad Christianity." He explains that a person is deemed "mad" or insane if the world that exists in his or her head does not connect with the world of reality. He goes on to show that for many Christians faith, God, Jesus and the world of the miraculous exist only in their heads and fail to intersect with daily living. These people's faith resembles madness because it stays aloof from reality, removed from the details of living. Faith is "mad" when it exists in my mind but does not touch the real world.[3]

Real-world faith pursues involvement with the world. We express our faith in the way we live our daily lives. We apply biblical stories and the principles they teach to the moral and ethical dilemmas of our day. The complex issues and problems in our world call for Christians who live like the Old Testament men of Issachar, understanding our times and knowing how the church should respond (1 Chron 12:32).

If Christianity Is Relevant

If Christian faith really matters in our world, it will affect our worldview because it will thrust us into the world. Once propelled into the world, we find ourselves asking, "What does it mean to be a follower of Jesus in a culture that is passively ignorant of him or aggressively hostile toward him?" How do we live for Jesus in a world opposed to his kingdom values? Consider four challenges of relating Christianity to our world.

Evangelism. In the United States one might get the impression that the primary desire of conservative Christians is to see the moral principles of Christian living applied to society at large—without actually seeing people come to personal faith in Christ.

We say we believe that transformation comes through changed lives in Christ, but we relate our faith to the world by implying that our real goal is the promotion of specific morals and values—regardless of others' Christian commitment. This drift represents a serious compromise of the gospel because it focuses on behavior rather than lives transformed by grace through faith in Christ.

Since the formation of the Moral Majority back in the 1980s, Christians' sense of mission has often gotten diluted into an advocacy of certain moral standards. Conservative groups like the Christian Coalition, Focus on the Family and others—as well as their liberal alternatives—give the impression that the real goal is to change laws and political systems, without the neces-sary first step of changed lives.

Addressing this issue, Luis Palau writes, "Proclamation of the gospel was Paul's primary course of action to confront and change a pagan society." Although most of us believe this—that the gospel has the power to change lives and therefore socie-ties—we fail to act on it. Here is Palau again:

Our doubt shows up in our priorities, in our agenda to change society. There's little enthusiasm for evangelism. Political action, yes. Public protest, yes. Open and vigorous soul-win-ning, no. We are no longer using the gospel as a tool to change America. Very few churches—even Bible-believing, evan-gelical churches—are seeing souls saved. We're not concen-trating on converting people. . . . The biblical way to transform society is to lead people to Jesus Christ and disciple them, one at a time.[4]

Engagement. I asked several dozen people at church how they interpreted Matthew 16:18—"Upon this rock I will build my church; and the gates of hell shall not prevail against it" (the King James Version that many of us heard from childhood). The replies generally went like this: "I think it means that we will be safe from Satan's attack."

I noted that this is indeed the promise of 1 John 4:4 ("the one who is in you is greater than the one who is in the world"); God will protect us. Then I explained that Matthew 16:18 is in no way a defensive statement promising that we will be safe from outside attack. Instead it is an offensive statement: the captives that Satan holds in his kingdom will not be safe from *our* "attack." As God's people, we boldly take the offensive, going out into the world to snatch Satan's captives away from him. God calls us to engagement (a military term) and to storming the gates of hell in Jesus' name. With this perspective, we become the "church militant."

The initial responses of my friends at church reflect the typical pattern of the Christian church, at least the church in middle-class America. We have moved, in George Hunter's words, from being "fishers of men" to being "keepers of the aquarium."[5] We shy away from engagement. We move out of our cities, pull our children out of public school systems, build our own Christian universities. Then we move even further away from engagement by developing Christian music (and criticizing those who attempt "crossover" into the secular market), Christian radio stations and Christian stores—all implicitly designed to keep us away from the negative aspects of our culture.

Christian media, music and institutions often start as tools for the better equipping of the people of God, but such disengagement implies a move toward privatized faith and irrelevant

Christianity if we forget the goal—to strengthen the saints so that they may be sent back out into the world as salt and light, or, in Paul's terms, as those who transmit the "aroma of Christ" (2 Cor 2:15) to our world.

Engagement means studying the issues of our day and interacting with them biblically. Engagement means involvement; there is no room to hide in the church or in our private safety zones. If we act as the people of God, we will infiltrate this world with his love and values; this means rubbing shoulders with secularists, humanists, pluralists and ordinary sinners like ourselves. Why? So that they might see Reality (another word for Truth) lived out in relevant ways through us.

One of the problems of engagement, however, is time. We often get so caught up in activities in our church or Christian fellowship that we unintentionally marginalize ourselves from the world. Bob Lupton, a Christian worker in urban Atlanta, writes about how we become "unneighborly neighbors."

Do strong loyalties to church necessitate disengagement from those who live next door? If so, I have a misconception of the role of the Christian in this world. I have understood the historic mission of the Church to be a proactive force, armed with vulnerable love, infiltrating every strata of society, transforming fallen people and systems through the power of the Spirit. It is tempting to allow the local church body to become our enclave of like-minded friends that provides a protective haven from the daily bombardment of destructive values. Yet engagement—not withdrawal—has always been the operative word of the Church militant. And love of one's neighbor remains its fundamental tactic.[6]

Integration. In conversations with a number of people who have no Christian commitment, I asked, "Who do you see as an authentic Christian in the world today?" One of them mentioned Billy Graham, but all the others identified the nun of Calcutta's slums, Mother Teresa. Why? "Because she lives out her faith in the way that Jesus would."

These people were not commenting on Mother Teresa's theology. They were simply identifying her integrated lifestyle. She lives out her faith. Her belief system results in outreach to the poorest of the poor in Calcutta. Her worldview and her daily life connect.

We say that we believe "Jesus is the answer" to the strife in our world. When we believe this, our worldview enlarges because we start grappling with how issues of faith apply to our modern world. How do we as Christians respond to AIDS, racism, environmental issues or euthanasia? What does it mean to be a Christian in a secular or pluralistic society?

John Stott exhorts the Christian community to integrated faith in his two-volume work *Involvement* (published also under the title *Issues Facing Christians Today*). In volume 1, *Being a Responsible Christian in a Non-Christian Society,* he encourages our full involvement in society, addressing issues like the nuclear threat, the environment, economic inequalities and human rights. In the second volume, *Social and Sexual Relationships in the Modern World,* he tackles more tough questions like unemployment, racism, poverty, feminism, marriage and divorce, abortion, and homosexuality. In short, Stott urges every Christian toward an integrated faith that grapples with the true questions of our time.[7]

An integrated faith and life expands our witness. My wife and I have had opportunities to proclaim Christ to others by explaining our biblical convictions about environmental issues. When people become aware that our faith relates to rain-forest destruction in Brazil and the extinction of species, they often want to hear why we believe what we believe, which leads to opportunities to share the gospel.

The same is true when we address human rights issues, economic injustices and world hunger. Believing that our faith is relevant to our world, we try to understand how God wants us to respond to these issues. When we articulate a biblical response to these issues, people are more inclined to ask about our faith.

Agents of hope. Lesslie Newbigin, in *The Gospel in a Pluralist Society,* writes, "The distinguishing mark of [the Christian] community will be hope." In a world suffocating in hopelessness, meaninglessness and despair, our mission is to build hope and a sense of positive anticipation. We present Jesus as hope because, quoting Newbigin again, this hope "is the oxygen of the soul."[8]

Stuart McAllister, a leader with Operation Mobilization in Europe and now head of the European Evangelical Alliance, caught the vision of the need for Christians to be agents of hope in postmodern society. Through a team of churches and ministries working together, McAllister and his associates have initiated an aggressive outreach called "Hope for Europe." Addressing many strata of society through a host of means, they are seeking to respond to the despair and meaninglessness left over from world wars as well as the tumultuous economic, social and political changes of the 1980s and 1990s. Thousands of Christians are banding together to infiltrate European society with the Jesus-centered message of hope. Their goal is to say to an entire region that God has a "hope and a future" for them (Jer 29:11).

Vincent Donovan went as an agent of hope to the nomadic

Masai people of East Africa. Through many struggles and lessons in crosscultural adaptation (summarized in his book *Christianity Rediscovered*), he lived and ministered with people who feared change of any kind, feared evil spirits and feared death. He points out, in fact, that the Masai language has no future tense. By presenting Jesus Christ, the hope of the present and the future, Donovan addressed their fears of change, evil and death. He summarizes, "I think you could say that one of the purposes and goals of evangelizing the Masai is to put a future tense in their language."[9]

Agents of Hope

How do our actions serve to give people a future tense?

Vivian acted as an agent of hope for Jeffrey. Though she is unmarried, she believes that her God-given mission is to serve foster children. One day a social worker brought Vivian a three-month-old boy, Jeffrey. He had been born a crack baby, addicted through his birth mother to crack cocaine. Through perseverance, Vivian loved this listless little boy to health. She went through a legal battle with the state and finally won the opportunity to adopt him. Vivian literally gave Jeffrey a new life, a future tense, hope. And as he learns from Vivian about the love of Jesus, she prays that he will come to faith in the Ultimate Hope.

Mimi and her husband, Kevin, prepare for missionary service to West Africa, in a country where hope is in short supply. Kevin currently volunteers in a ministry at church where he serves as a "big brother" to young boys, most of whom do not have dads at home. Mimi counsels on a suicide hotline, helping people in total despair find hope.

Zac Niringiye and fellow leaders of FOCUS, a college-age

ministry in Uganda, act out their commitment to be Christ's agents of hope in a country devastated by HIV/AIDS (Uganda has one of the highest percentages of HIV/AIDS cases in the world). He says, "Several years ago we decided that AIDS is not a social challenge; AIDS is a challenge to the church." So FOCUS has established ministries to serve the families of those with HIV/AIDS. In spite of opposition—even from other Christians who thought the disease was "God's judgment on sinful behavior"—they moved forward.

They offer proactive public health prevention, counseling to the bereaved and support for thousands of children who have lost parents to the disease. They work to give their country a "future and a hope" through the demonstrated love of Jesus.

World Changers

In our church we sing a song, "I Want to Be a History-Maker," which states our desire "to be God's pen on history's pages." The song catches the transformational spirit that Marx predicted for those who lived by his *Communist Manifesto:* "The philosophers have only interpreted the world; the point is to change it."

History has shown that Marx could not change the world, but Jesus did. And he continues to change it through his people, the church. As we imitate Daniel in Babylonia, Joseph in Egypt and Esther in Persia, we can influence our society and our world toward positive gospel change.

Our faith addresses the real issues of our world. Nothing matters more.

Next Steps

1. Think through your schedule over the next week, and look for two or three ways that you can actively engage your faith.

2. Look through the Sunday newspaper and identify several national or international issues that interest you. Then think through (either alone or with a small group of friends), "How could I/we be an 'agent of hope' in each of these situations?"

8

• • • • • • •

DO I BELIEVE THAT GOD WANTS TO USE MY LIFE?

This man is my chosen instrument to carry my name before the Gentiles and their kings and before the people of Israel. (Acts 9:15)

Have you ever felt insignificant? Too small to make a difference in this immense world of need? Lisa's response to the challenge of becoming a world-aware Christian might sound familiar: "I chose to narrow my worldview because knowledge of the world overwhelmed me. I can scarcely manage my own life; how can I be concerned about affecting the world?"

Perhaps nothing will shrink our worldview faster than a sense of being overwhelmed by the needs of our world:

☐ urban violence

☐ 1.1 billion people in China

☐ almost a billion starving, hungry or homeless people worldwide

☐ unreached Hindus and Muslims

☐ daily crises brought to our attention by news broadcasts and newspapers

The vastness of need is dizzying. Aware of our limitations, we want to shrink back like turtles into the protective shell of a smaller worldview.

But then we come to the Scriptures and discover a God who desires that his glory be declared among the nations (Ps 96:3). We see his willingness, "not wanting anyone to perish, but everyone to come to repentance" (2 Pet 3:9; also 1 Tim 2:4). And we hear his call to respond to need and be his witnesses to the ends of the earth (see Is 6:1-8; Mt 9:36-38; Acts 1:8).

Do we believe in a personal God who uses broken, limited and overwhelmed people to do his will in the earth? Do we believe in the God of "mustard seed" faith, who does great things through what appear to be insignificant means? Do we believe Paul's words to the Corinthians, that God chooses "the foolish things of the world to shame the wise . . . the weak things of the world to shame the strong . . . the lowly things of this world and the despised things . . . to nullify the things that are" (1 Cor 1:27-28)?

The sense of being overwhelmed has reduced many Christians to functional agnostics. We have personal faith, but we do not see God's purposes for us. We live our lives saying, in effect, "I believe in God, but I have no idea of how he wants to work through me."

The Biblical Affirmation

If you see yourself as small, insignificant or overwhelmed, take courage: you are exactly the humble kind of person that God wants to use mightily in the world. Peter wrote to encourage

Christians, " 'God opposes the proud but gives grace to the humble.' Humble yourselves, therefore, under God's mighty hand, that he may lift you in due time" (1 Pet 5:5-6).

Consider how the Bible illustrates this God-will-use-you-no-matter-how-small-you-feel affirmation throughout. The small, the insignificant, the "mustard seeds," the obscure: these are the chosen instruments of God. God selected the people of Israel based on his love, not based on their size or power (Deut 7:7-8). In his grace, God thinned out the forces under Gideon from thirty-two thousand to three hundred so that it would be clear to all that God had won the battle (Judg 7:1—8:12). In his grace, God made Saul—who was small in his own eyes—the great king of Israel, but when Saul became self-sufficient and disobedient, God brought him down (1 Sam 15:17).

In the New Testament nothing illustrates God's perspective on insignificant people better than the Christmas story. The famous people of those days receive only a passing reference. Luke alludes to Caesar Augustus and Quirinius to give readers a sense of the historical setting (Lk 2:1-3), but then, writing under the inspired direction of the Holy Spirit, he focuses on the world-changing people in the Christmas story:

☐ Mary and Joseph, peasants chosen by God to bear the Messiah and raise him as their son (vv. 4-7)

☐ shepherds, occupants of the lowest social stratum of society, chosen by God to be the first to hear that God had fulfilled his promise and brought a Savior (vv. 8-20)

☐ Simeon and Anna, elderly people who went unnoticed by the daily mobs in Jerusalem, but whom God singled out as among the first to recognize that the Messiah had come (vv. 21-38)

The New Testament also provides us with a negative illustration in the Corinthian church. In opposition to humility, the Corinthians wanted status. Paul wrote to affirm to them that God, contrary to their drive for status, uses the small, the weak, the powerless, the insignificant to change the world. Why? So that the work done will clearly be seen as the work of God, so that no one might boast except in the Lord (1 Cor 1:29-30).

Whom Does God Use?

Oswald J. Smith founded the People's Church in Toronto, a globally minded congregation that has significantly influenced the world mission of the church for over fifty years. During his tenure as pastor Smith wrote many books, among them an answer to our question entitled *The Man God Uses.* Today the book would be retitled *The Person God Uses,* but it still speaks to the basic question we all have: If I desire to be used as an instrument of the purposes of God, how do I qualify? What are the characteristics of the person used by God?

God uses our availability. Perhaps the most famous biblical account of a person being called out by God occurs in Isaiah 6:1-8. Isaiah lives in a time of turmoil—the powerful King Uzziah has just died, and Isaiah's world will change. In the midst of such turbulence, Isaiah has a vision of God. He sees God's glory, confronts his own sinfulness, experiences God's forgiveness. Then he hears God's call: "Whom shall I send? And who will go for us?"

Isaiah makes himself available to God. He says, "Here I am, Lord. Send me!" There is no presumptuousness here—after all, Isaiah has just come face to face with the awesomeness of God and the awfulness of his own sin. He is simply expressing his availability—"I do not know what I have to offer, Lord, but here I am."

A key ingredient in our worldview, if we desire God to use our lives for his greater purposes, is the understanding that God uses ordinary people who make themselves available to him. Comprehending this allows us to enter the world with hope. As we remember the biblical accounts of how God changed the world through cowards, shepherds and impulsive fishermen, we will start asking, "OK, Lord, how do you want to use me in this broken world?"

William Carey, sometimes called the father of modern missions, made himself available to God from his cobbler's bench in late-eighteenth-century England. In spite of opposition from others, he sailed to India as a missionary. His availability to God yielded wonderful results for the kingdom of Christ:

> When he died, after more than forty years of ministry in India, he had translated the Bible into three major Indian languages, had founded what has become the largest newspaper in India, had established the strong and effective Baptist Church Union in India, had founded what has become the largest seminary in India, and had done more than any individual to bring the message of the Gospel of Christ to that subcontinent. He was one simple cobbler who took God at his word, and his obedience immeasurably affected an entire subcontinent.[1]

Stephanie made herself available to God in a similar way. God directed her into an outreach ministry to international students from the People's Republic of China. Rather than being overwhelmed by the volume of people in China (1.1 billion), she focused on God's ability to use her life for his kingdom in the lives of a few people.

Using her gifts of hospitality to provide a comfortable environment where the gospel could be presented, she developed dozens of friendships with PRC students. After several years, many of the students she befriended had returned to China, and they asked Stephanie to come visit.

Having traveled only seldom, Stephanie considered China a big trip, but she again rendered herself available to God, and she went. Over the course of five weeks she visited over twenty of her friends across China. In spite of sickness and a trip to a Beijing hospital, God used that visit to direct Stephanie to move to China as an English teacher. Now she touches lives in the enormous city of Beijing, once more making herself available to be used by God.

God uses our experiences. Ernie worked with his six brothers in the wholesale fruit and produce business. Their business prospered, and they agreed together to be generous—exceedingly generous as a matter of fact. As a result of this generosity, Ernie and his brothers knew many Christian leaders across the country, including Pat Robertson of the Christian Broadcasting Network—which explains the phone call.

The phone rang at about 10:45 on Saturday night. Christie and I had just returned home from a long trip culminating in forty hours of travel on the last two days. We were exhausted, but I answered the phone anyway.

"Hi Paul, this is Ernie."

"Ernie, what's up?"

"Well, I need your help. What shall I pack if I'm going to Zaire?"

"Wow," I said, "what a question! We're just back after a long trip. Can I call you back on this? When do you leave?"

"Tomorrow morning," he replied, so we decided that we had better talk. Ernie explained that he was flying in the morning via the Concorde to Paris, where he, Pat Robertson and a crew from the Christian Broadcasting Network would embark for Zaire on a private jet owned by President Mobutu. They would fly to Kinshasa to consult with the president and his chief ministers on a variety of issues. Ernie had been asked to come based on his years of experience with fruit and produce distribution.

Ernie and the crew flew to Kinshasa, and for the next seven days they met with cabinet ministers and eventually with President Mobutu himself. On the final day, Ernie stood on the presidential barge with President Mobutu cruising up the Congo River. He conversed through a translator with the president, one of the most powerful men of Africa. Ernie shared his testimony with President Mobutu and told him that repentance and transformation in Jesus Christ was the only hope for his country.

There must have been times in Ernie's past when he was loading and unloading fruit and produce and wondering, *Lord, why do you have me here?* He had desired greater evangelistic ministry, but God had kept him in the family business. But that day, as he stood with a man who could influence an entire continent for Jesus Christ, the years of fruit and produce distribution started to make sense. God was taking those years of cucumbers, zucchinis and potatoes and using Ernie's experiences for something unique.

Marion had a different story. After thirty-five years working as a coordinator of mass food preparation, first at a military base, then at a huge hospital, Marion retired. She asked, "God, how can you use me now?" and she started to research possibilities. After only five weeks of retirement, Marion departed on her first trip to Haiti, the poorest country in the Western Hemisphere, to work in food preparation for an orphanage. Her expertise helped increase the orphanage's efficiency, and over the next five months its capabilities expanded from feeding eight hundred children per week to feeding over two thousand.

And that was just the beginning. Ten years later, Marion is still at it, having made more than thirty trips to Haiti and now overseeing another orphanage. Her years in the food-preparation business continue to benefit hundreds of children in Haiti.

When we affirm the doctrine of the "sovereignty" of God, we state our belief in God's ability to work all things together for good (see Rom 8:28). Throughout the course of our lives, God sends or allows a host of experiences—experiences that we may never understand fully—which can then be mightily used for his purposes.

When we combine availability with experience, we say to God, "Here I am, Lord; how do you want to use my family background, my growing-up experiences, my education and my life background to benefit the work of Christ's kingdom here on earth?"

God uses our prayers. Philosopher Blaise Pascal once said, "God instituted prayer in order to lend to His creatures the dignity of causality." Pascal was affirming the biblical truth that God involves us in his global purposes through prayer. In some miraculous way God has limited himself to work through us and our prayers.

Jesus affirms this in Matthew 9:36-38. When confronted with overwhelming need—people who were "harassed and helpless, like sheep without a shepherd"—the disciples tended either to ignore the people or to ask Jesus to send them away (see a parallel passage in Mt 14:14-15). In contrast, Jesus responds with compassion, but he tells the disciples to pray; in the face of such oppressive needs, they should "ask the Lord of the harvest, therefore, to send out workers into his harvest field." In light of people's great distress and many needs, they must first acknowledge through prayer that the Lord of the harvest was in charge.

J. Christy Wilson affirmed this to me and other students at Gordon-Conwell Theological Seminary when he armed the prayer room with a Bible and a copy of the daily newspaper. He explained, "The Bible reminds us of the God of all times and all peoples; the newspaper reminds us of specific situations in the world where we need to ask for God's intervention."

My wife and I made two trips to South Africa in the early 1990s. We gained firsthand experience of the misery of the racial separation in that country. We were burdened, but we returned home uncertain of what we could do in the face of a massive apartheid government. But we knew we could pray. Both within and outside South Africa, God directed thousands to pray, and in 1993 the laws of apartheid came down.

In 1994, just nine days before South Africa's first democratic elections, key leaders in the country were divided. The news media expected a bloodbath because Chief Buthelezi of the Inkatha Freedom Party refused to participate in the elections and threatened anybody who did. But Christians around the world joined South African Christians in praying. And in the back rooms of a prayer rally in Natal, Buthelezi and Nelson Mandela ironed out their differences. On April 27, 1994, South Africa held free elections on a day that was violence-free.

Whatever the need, crisis or opportunity, we all can respond in prayer, believing that God listens and works through prayer. Our participation in the world and in current events increases dramatically when we reaffirm our commitment to pray. Even though we may not know the results until we get to heaven, we go to the God of history and ask him to intervene.

God uses our pain. Our church planned a "Global Awareness Week," and we asked every fellowship and every small group to host an international speaker. We assigned Krister Sairsingh, a Trinidadian man converted to Christ from Hinduism, to speak to the divorce-recovery support group.

About a week before the scheduled meeting, the leader of the support group called and asked to cancel: "We have so many hurting people, I don't think they can handle hearing about outreach and developing global concern."

Krister came up with the solution. He went to the group as scheduled, and he spoke on how God uses us in spite of our brokenness. Referring to 2 Corinthians 1:4, he reminded the group members that God comforts us in our pain "so that we can comfort those in any trouble with the comfort we ourselves have received from God."

As a result of Krister's encouragement, the group chose to "adopt" (through prayer, letters and gifts) a single mother of three serving as a missionary nurse and teacher in Angola. They knew that they could empathize with the challenges she faced, and they decided to play the part of home support for a fellow single parent.

Krister struck a nerve with a core biblical truth—that God can use even our pain for his sovereign purposes. In the Old Testament, God used Joseph, who had experienced abandonment, betrayal, captivity, imprisonment and a dysfunctional family, to achieve great purposes. Joseph later reminded his brothers, "You intended to harm me, but God intended it for good to accomplish what is now being done, the saving of many lives" (Gen 50:20).

In the New Testament, the ultimate example is Jesus. He endured suffering so that he might learn obedience (Heb 5:8). He experienced the wrenching pain of the cross, and he showed us how to endure suffering by keeping our eyes fixed on our eternal goal (Heb 12:1-3). Through his pain we have forgiveness and redemption and a new life. God used Jesus' pain so that we might have a gospel to preach to the nations.

In missions history, one of the classic stories of God's use of pain occurred in a leprosy colony on Molokai, one of the Hawaiian islands. Father Damien came to minister among these hopeless people, but he encountered little success. His ministry failed, and he decided to quit and return home. But before his departure, it was discovered that Father Damien had contracted leprosy. He could not leave.

The next Sunday, church services were full. The news of Father Damien's leprosy had circulated through the colony, and now the residents were coming to hear him preach. They knew that he understood what they were going through, and they wanted to see if, in the face of his own leprosy, he still had a message of hope. On that day his true ministry began, which led to the conversion of the majority of the colony.

Whenever we are tempted to think that we cannot make a difference in the world because of our painful past, or that our present difficulties disqualify us from being part of what God is doing in the world, we need to come back to Scripture, which asserts that God can turn pain into his avenue of grace and mercy. Our pain—past or present—may be a God-given avenue into a ministry that we could never undertake pain-free.

God uses our faith. The person desirous of being used by God must be willing to take some risks. That might entail reaching out to international students as Stephanie did, or talking to a powerful president as Ernie did, or daring to believe that God can use us in the midst of our pain as Krister did. Believing that God can use our lives involves faith, and faith involves risk.

A quotation attributed to Hudson Taylor, the pioneer missionary into China, says it best: "Unless there is an element of risk in our exploits for God, there is no need for faith."

For every person, risk and faith-based decisions take different shapes. For some it is crossing into a different cultural or racial section of the city to build friendships and get involved in outreach. For others it might mean stepping out in evangelistic witness in the workplace.

For my wife Christie, risk-taking faith means befriending people in her microbiology lab and trying to bring the hope of the gospel into the mundaneness of daily work. For Todd, risk-taking faith has meant using his financial skills to establish a small loan company to help the poor in a barrio of Mexico City. For Sandra, risk-taking faith has meant applying her administrative skills to the management of an inner-city soup kitchen. For David, risk-taking faith has taken him in the service of World Vision International into places like Bosnia and Rwanda at the height of their conflicts. For the Bishop family, risk-taking faith has taken the whole family out in short-term missionary service.

God uses people who step out in faith, who leave their comfort zones and say, "God, I'll get involved if you give me the courage, strength and endurance I need." And when we venture forward in risk-taking faith, God meets us there!

An Addendum to Hebrews 11

Maybe it's time to reread Hebrews 11. In this survey of the "Hall of Fame" of faith, we find some pretty seedy characters. We meet Moses the murderer, Abraham the liar, Jacob the deceiver, Gideon the coward and David the adulterer/liar/murderer. Rahab the prostitute is included, as is Samson the compromiser.

These people God holds forth as examples. These men and women constitute the "great cloud of witnesses" (Heb 12:1) designed to inspire us to endurance and faith in the face of overwhelming odds and opposition.

What is God's message to us here? Is it that we are to imitate these people's weaknesses? By no means! Instead, God illustrates his actions through these people to remind us that when there is faith, he can work past our defects.

The God who influenced Egypt through Joseph, Babylonia through Daniel, Nineveh through Jonah and the world through Paul—this is our God. The needs of the world are overwhelming, but we have an *awesome* God, a God who will do his work through people like you and me.

God—through us—is writing an addendum to Hebrews 11.

Next Steps

1. Look over your next week's schedule and determine one place where you can take a risk of faith—through speaking up for the gospel, or giving a service, or giving a financial gift. Then take the risk and offer your action up to God, praying, "Lord, this little gift, this mustard seed, I offer up to you, asking that you will make it something great for the sake of the kingdom of Christ."

2. List your gifts, experiences and other resources that you could offer to the work of God worldwide. Pause and ask God, "Where and how can you use these in the service of your kingdom around the world?" Then take action by writing a letter, sending an e-mail message or making a call to someone (a pastor, friend, Christian worker) who might give you some ideas on finding opportunities to serve, either short-term or long-term.

9
• • • • • • •

WHOSE AGENDA WILL I LIVE BY?

*Why do you call me, "Lord,
Lord," and do not do what I say?*
(Luke 6:46)

If being a Christian affected only my eternal destiny—"I'm
saved and forgiven and bound for heaven"—then being a Christian would not be difficult. But by his death for our sins Jesus
not only purchased our forgiveness and a place in heaven. He
also purchased our lives; we have been "bought at a price"
(1 Cor 6:20). He establishes himself in our lives as Savior *and*
as Lord.

Dangerous Question 6, the agenda question, strikes at the
issue of lordship: who maintains control over my life? If I
profess to follow Christ, it means giving him free rein in my life.

Some want to live as "Jesus in my back pocket" Christians.
We walk through life with an open-in-case-of-emergency relationship with Jesus. We call on him as needed, but we do not

make decisions or set priorities with an absolute devotion to him as our Master. Jesus is convenience rather than absolute Lord.

Those who choose to live by their own agenda can tolerate behavior and attitudes that keep their worldview narrow and self-serving. Their self-centered agenda can include racist attitudes and feelings of cultural superiority. They may be able to convince themselves that they do not really need to care much about people outside their normal sphere of influence.

Are these people even Christians? That question can be settled only by God, the final Judge, but one thing is clear. Living by our own agenda indicates that we have misunderstood the claims of Jesus, and at least discipleship, if not salvation, is out of the question. The demands of discipleship—like taking up our cross daily and denying ourselves (Lk 9:23)—concern only those who understand that Jesus is Lord.

When we submit ourselves to Jesus' agenda, our worldview changes and enlarges. Suddenly we find him calling us to care for the socially rejected—our modern-day lepers, Samaritans or prostitutes. He stirs us to reach out to people from other cultures, other ethnic groups, other worlds. With Jesus as Lord, we recognize the diversity of the world and the people that he has created, and our behavior changes accordingly.

My wife and I recently had the privilege of visiting with Caesar Molebatsi, a Christian leader from South Africa. Caesar lost his leg thirty years ago when a white driver ran over him, dragged him and his bicycle a distance of fifty yards, and left him for dead.

After recovering, Caesar lived for retaliation. He set his heart on hurting or killing that man. But to his surprise, in the process of avenging his pain Caesar came to know Jesus Christ as his Lord and Savior. Suddenly everything changed. Caesar realized that he had no option facing him but to obey Jesus, forgive the man and release his desire to retaliate. As difficult as it was, he faced the man and forgave him—because Caesar had decided to submit himself to Jesus' agenda, which commanded him to love his enemies and forgive.

Priority Questions

If Dangerous Question 1—who is Jesus?—is the most important objective, theological question we have considered, Question 6—whose agenda will I live by?—is the most important subjective, personal question. No matter how we answer the other questions, true life change (or worldview change) will be limited if we do not make Jesus our Lord.

Howard A. Snyder cites as the number-one element for building a biblical kingdom worldview "unconditional faith in Jesus Christ and obedience to his commands and to the moral law of God as revealed in Scripture."[1] Instructing readers on what he calls "the Great Commission life-style," Robert Coleman writes, "Obedience to Christ is the final test of our love."[2]

Beliefs can be isolated to a compartment of our minds. The Bible tells us that even the demons believe that there is one God (Jas 2:19), but they are still demons! True faith affects every area of our lives. If we love Jesus, if we desire to make him Lord, if we agree to live by his agenda, then our beliefs take shape in dedicated obedience and a commitment to keep his commands.

If Jesus Is Lord

What does "living by Jesus' agenda" look like? Do I just sit and wait for Jesus to tell me what to do? Robertson McQuilkin says no: "Obedience to God is never fulfilled through mere passive availability."[3]

Making Jesus' agenda our agenda requires active, conscious decisions to follow him. If Jesus is Lord, we open our hands before him and present ourselves as "living sacrifices" who are committed to being transformed by his worldview for us, rather than conformed to a self-centered worldview dictated to us by the world (Rom 12:1-2).

If Jesus is Lord, we release to him our rights. Today's Western Christians tend to take on the culture's sense of perceived "entitlements." Many of us think we have the right to ask God for safety, comfort and even happiness. We want God to respond to our needs—and thus we try to reduce the almighty, sovereign God to a cosmic Santa who will coddle us on his knee and grant our every wish.

Releasing our rights to Jesus means giving over our lives. It requires us to identify those things that we think are due us: good health, prosperity, long life, a house in the suburbs, a vacation home at the lake, a job where we will feel fulfilled, a spouse, a family. Having identified these things, we place each of them, one by one, on God's altar. In other words, we fully acknowledge our dreams before the Lord Jesus, but we no longer see them as rights or prerequisites for obedience.

Even Jesus struggled with this, so take heart. Yet at the moment of his greatest desire to abandon God's plan and preserve himself, he released his rights and prayed, "Not my will, but yours be done" (Lk 22:42).

I admire Allison, who chose a profession loaded with cultural entitlements and rights. She studied to become a medical doctor, attending a school where many classmates spoke openly of their dreams of making huge sums of money. Rather than succumbing to the pressure to follow suit, Allison decided to invite the Lord Jesus to guide her career moves.

Laying aside her perceived rights and her earning potential, she followed Jesus into work with the poor, serving as a doctor at an urban health clinic. It is not the safest neighborhood, and Allison's salary would be laughed at by her classmates. But obedience to Jesus' agenda requires us to release our attachments to safety and prosperity.

Allison understands what it means to hear God's call.

There is only one place to begin [to hear God's call]. One who does not acknowledge the absolute lordship of Christ in every choice of life cannot hear any call from God. . . . If Jesus Christ alone is absolute Lord of my life, He alone has the right to make the greatest of all choices for me: how will I invest my life?[4]

Dick and Marjorie Winchell released their rights in another way. As a middle-aged couple, they actively released their children to the service of Christ abroad. They knew that this would mean times of loneliness and longing for their family members, but when their children were still young Marjorie and Dick had prayed, "Lord, we ask that we won't get to meet our grandchildren until our children are home on their first furlough from overseas crosscultural service."

Releasing our rights takes many shapes. For some it means extra generosity, releasing the right to spend extra, hard-earned money on themselves and giving it instead to the work of the Lord Jesus Christ. For others it means invested time, using days off or vacation time to serve others. Some release the right to pursue marriage and use their singleness as a privileged position for maximum service to Christ (see Mt 19:12; 1 Cor 7:32). Others release the right to a quiet home in the country and move into a city neighborhood to bring the peace of Christ into an area overlooked by the church.

If Jesus is Lord, we release to him our biases, prejudices and racism. Perhaps the greatest hindrance to true revival in our communities and cities lies in our failure to see others with the grace of Christ. Rather than looking at people through Jesus' eyes of compassion, we resort to cultural or racial stereotypes.

A young man in Myanmar (Burma) illustrated this point powerfully. This young man came from the north of the country and was part of the Karen ethnic minority. We were in a seminar together, and on Saturday morning we were all supposed to go into the capital city, Yangon, to participate in open-air outreach meetings. The young man refused to go. He explained to me through a translator, "Most of the people in this city are Burmese, and the Burmese have historically oppressed my people. If I witness to them, one of them might get saved, and I don't want that to happen because I don't want there to be any Burmese in heaven."

His words shocked me. I had never heard such a blatant statement of ethnic hostility. I appealed to him based on the sacrifice of Christ—that God so loved *the world* that he gave us Jesus. Thankfully, the young man changed his mind, realizing that his bias and cultural bitterness could not be maintained if he was submitted to the lordship of Christ.

This experience triggered many thoughts about my own life. Do my biases ever keep me from witnessing

☐ to someone from another ethnic group?

☐ to those whose work I hate—clinicians at an abortion center, or manufacturers of cigarettes, or distributors of alcohol?

☐ to a person with a physical or mental handicap?

☐ to someone with radically different political views from mine?

☐ to a homeless person or someone in shabby clothing?

□ to a drug addict or an alcoholic?
□ to those who are ostentatiously rich and proud?
□ to those in the gay community?

Releasing my biases takes diligent work and honest conversation with God, asking for his power to overcome attitudes that may have been formed through family values, bad experiences or simple ignorance. But living under the lordship of Christ requires that we let these biases go so that we might be freed to love each person as Christ loved us.

If Jesus is Lord, we release to him our expectations. A recent conversation with a sixty-eight-year-old Christian brother illustrated to me what it means to live under the lordship of Christ. Rather than discussing his retirement plans (a normal topic for sixty-eight-year-olds), he described how God had led him to minister in an enormous Third World city. I asked him if he had ever considered retiring.

"Well," he said, "I suppose I could retire, but I'm not really sure that the model of retirement I see in the United States is a biblical model." Rather than pursuing a way of life that our culture considers normal, he made submitting himself to the Lord his first priority.

Francis Xavier was the Jesuit director of missions in India, China and Japan in the sixteenth century. He wrote back to Europe that he would like to return to Paris and "go shouting up and down the streets to tell the students to give up their small ambitions and come eastward to preach the Gospel of Christ."[5]

Expectations come out when I hear a student say, "Well, after I have done [this or that], I'll get serious about following Jesus." Expectations are revealed when a person makes it obvious that they would never consider serving Jesus Christ outside their current safe environment.

Expectations derailed the rich young ruler. He had followed the Jewish law from childhood, but Jesus gave a command that he could not follow. Jesus saw into his heart and instructed him to rewrite his personal agenda. He confronted the young man's material comforts and expectations of security. When Jesus told him to release these expectations and follow him, the young man retreated sorrowfully. When his own expectations and Jesus' command came into conflict, he chose his desire for security (Mt 19:16-22; Lk 18:18-23).

When Jesus is Lord, we place ourselves at his disposal as witnesses—willing to go out into our Jerusalem, Judea, Samaria and the uttermost parts of the earth (Acts 1:8). Our desires and expectations certainly play a part in our decision-making—for God does work through our natural inclinations—but the overriding value is the lordship of Jesus. When his agenda for us conflicts with our agenda (or the agenda of others) for ourselves, will we obey the Lord?

If Jesus is Lord, we release to him our future. The Old Testament heroine Esther found herself in a difficult position. She had been chosen to become queen of Persia even though she was a Hebrew. Her people faced annihilation, and she could intervene to try to spare them; but her attempt could cost her own life, because no one spoke to the king without his invitation and permission.

Nevertheless, Esther released her future to the God she trusted, and she broke protocol. Believing that she had been raised up for "such a time as this" (Esther 4:14), she initiated the conversation and made her request, fully resolved concerning her own future: "If I perish, I perish" (4:16). Her courageous act saved her people.

In the early twentieth century the Student Volunteer Movement rose up among young people committed to the Great Commission. Desiring to evangelize the world in their own generation, they lived with an open-handedness toward their future. With members committing themselves to "planning to go [overseas] but willing to stay [home]," the Student Volunteer Movement produced hundreds of new missionaries and thousands of dedicated home supporters.

The strength of the Student Volunteer Movement was its members' common pledge to say before God, "Because I am totally resolved to the lordship of Christ, I release my future into his care, planning on pursuing the more difficult choice but obedient to wherever he wants me."

Who Is the Master?

Tony Campolo writes, "The greatest danger to those who would follow Jesus is not overt persecution from society, but subtle seduction by its values. Compromise with the culture has always had more potential for annihilating true faith than has intellectual skepticism or the threat of being thrown to the lions."[6]

Exhorting believers to sexual purity and physical control, Paul the apostle wrote, " 'Everything is permissible for me'—but not everything is beneficial. 'Everything is permissible for me'—but I will not be mastered by anything" (1 Cor 6:12). Implication? Whatever masters us holds the reins of our lives. When Paul says, "I will not be mastered by anything," he recommits himself to Jesus' agenda.

Jesus alone will be the Master. My worldview, my behavior with others, my priorities and my choices will come under one umbrella—the umbrella of the lordship of Jesus Christ.

Whose agenda are you living by?

Next Steps

Think through your own life and your future. Then, bringing everything before Jesus, go through and actively release to him

☐ your rights—regarding marital status, family, earning potential, home, career track and the like

☐ your biases, prejudices or racism—confess any thoughts of superiority you've had, and ask Jesus to fill you with his love

☐ your expectations—actively "give up your small ambitions" and ask the Lord Jesus to fill you with his dreams for your life

10
• • • • • • •

HOW'S
YOUR
WORLDVIEW?

Once more Jesus put his hands
on the man's eyes. Then
his eyes were opened, his sight
was restored, and he
saw everything clearly.
(Mark 8:25)

This book opened with an explanation of the significance of worldview and how it affects our perspective on ourselves, our faith, our world and our roles in the world. Now the questions are out in the open. Will you let your worldview be changed so that it becomes aligned with God's?

In a letter to concerned supporters, Bob Seiple, president of World Vision U.S.A., appealed for bigger worldviews in the body of Christ: "Isolation is not a moral option for America. Here the church must hold our government accountable. Our thinking has to be global, our vision clear, and hopes transcendent. The world that 'God so loved' demands today the involvement modeled by a Son who would freely give His all."[1]

But even if you have gained new dedication to answer the Six Dangerous Questions from a biblical framework, you may still be looking for ways to apply the principles in daily living. Consider the following ideas, and select a few to integrate into your life.

Bigger Worldviews and the Way We Pray
☐ Start praying for people in your sphere of influence who have no knowledge of Jesus Christ as their Lord and Savior.

☐ Pray that God will give you a new dream of how he wants to influence the world through your experiences, your career, your pain.

☐ Pray for courage to yield your life to Jesus as Lord—releasing your rights and expectations and future to him.

☐ Pray through some of the greatest challenges of our times—abortion, euthanasia, ecology, the gap between the rich and poor—and ask God for wisdom to understand how to apply biblical truth and the gospel of Jesus Christ to these issues.

☐ Every time you change clothes, pray for the countries cited on your clothing labels. Use all of those "Made in Hong Kong" and "Assembled in India" labels as reminders to pray around the world.

☐ Choose one country and start to pray for it every day. Get a copy of Patrick Johnstone's *Operation World* so that you can pray intelligently about the spiritual condition and needs of that country.

Bigger Worldviews and the Things We Learn
☐ Study your own geographic area in an effort to identify pockets of people who have no apparent knowledge of or faith in Jesus Christ.

□ Build a partnership between your church and another church outside your cultural, ethnic or socioeconomic group in an effort to understand the glorious diversity of the body of Christ.

□ Learn a foreign language so that you can build bridges between yourself and people from other cultures or ethnic groups.

□ Study one particular issue (like environmental concerns or tensions in the Middle East) or area of the world (like Muslim North Africa or Central Asia) so that you can help fellow Christians pray more intelligently about it. Choose something or somewhere that really interests you. Start researching by clipping articles, surfing the Internet or going to the library.

□ Subscribe to at least one magazine from a mission agency dedicated to pioneering outreach (going to places where people are hearing about Jesus for the first time).

□ Buy an up-to-date world map and memorize the country names so that you know where your neighbors live in the global village. (Can you find the United States on a map of the world?)

Bigger Worldviews and the People We Touch

□ Pray for people with whom you work, study or live, and ask God for an opportunity to talk with them about some worldview issues—like the reality of heaven and hell, the uniqueness of Jesus or Christianity's relevance to the issues of daily life.

□ Find out about at least one of the people your church supports in crosscultural ministry overseas. Send that person a letter, a fax or an e-mail message so that you can learn more about his or her ministry situation, needs and prayer requests.

□ Invite an international student home for a meal and start a friendship.

□ Study the basic teachings of another world religion so that you can demonstrate respect to people of other faiths and address the gospel of Jesus Christ to the teachings of that faith.

□ Visit a church where the Christian faith is celebrated in a cultural style or language different from your own. Then read Revelation 7:9, realizing that you have just had a preview of the worship of heaven.

□ Visit a Muslim mosque or a Hindu temple so that you can start wrestling with what it means to present Jesus Christ to adherents of that religion.

Bigger Worldviews and the Risks We Take

□ Open your mouth in witness and affirm what you believe to others—about Jesus, about God's call on your life, about heaven or about the biblical concept of justice.

□ Volunteer for a service opportunity that you know you can fulfill only if God grants you the particular strength and ability to do so.

□ Initiate a friendship with an international student or a person of another culture or ethnic group in an effort to break out of your limited perspective.

□ Get out of your comfort zone in service. Put yourself in a "must trust" environment, a place where you know you must trust God for safety or effectiveness or ability to accomplish the task before you.

□ Get involved in some current issue—social, political, economic—and study the Scriptures in an effort to integrate your personal faith with this issue.

□ Take a risk—a generous financial gift, a crosscultural

outreach opportunity, a short-term mission trip—anything that you can do to say, in effect, "I am actively affirming that I believe in heaven and I'm committed to living with an eternal perspective."

Why Bigger Worldviews?

Peter Kuzmic of Croatia offers this challenge:

We are challenged today by a modernized recasting of Tertullian's question: What has Boston to do with Bosnia? . . .

Why should we concern ourselves with the human tragedies of Bosnia, Somalia, and Bangladesh? Why should the holocaust taking place in Rwanda touch our lives when it is obvious that the sovereign Lord has placed us so as to be secure from those dangers and other winds of adversity? Should we worry about restoring democracy to Haiti, ask questions about human rights in China, or be concerned with the plight of human emigrants?

Why should we burden ourselves with the burdens of the world and allow [ourselves] to be disturbed by statistics of war, disease, and poverty? Why should the turmoil of the world disrupt the tranquility of our hearts and surrounding?

May I suggest that there is only one compelling reason— "For God so loved the world."[2]

In response to this love, will we forge a faith that takes on the challenges of our world with energy and zeal? In light of Jesus' sacrifice, will we expand our outreach to include people outside our normal cultural, social, economic or ethnic framework? Because of the compassion of Christ, will we deepen our faith so that we are willing to step outside of our comfort zone?

The answer resounds "Yes!" if we understand

☐ that Jesus is the only Savior

☐ that heaven and hell are real

☐ that our world needs people who will address the gospel to the issues and crises of the day

☐ that God wants to use our lives

☐ that Jesus Christ is Lord

Dangerous questions lead to dangerous answers. And dangerous answers transform our worldview. Take courage and live out your answers!

Notes

Chapter 1: What's a Worldview?
[1]Peter Cotterell, *Mission and Meaninglessness* (London: S.P.C.K., 1990), p. 25.
[2]Sam Wilson and Gordon Aeschliman, *The Hidden Half* (Pasadena, Calif.: MARC, n.d.), p. 97.
[3]*Leadership*, Fall 1995, p. 54.
[4]Leith Anderson, "The Turn Inward," *Leadership*, Fall 1995, pp. 98-100.

Chapter 2: Worldview & Crosscultural Involvement
[1]K. N. Panikkar, "Globalization and Culture," *The Hindu*, October 4, 1995.
[2]Ibid.

Chapter 3: The Separation of Intellect & Lifestyle
[1]Peter Cotterell, *Mission and Meaninglessness* (London: S.P.C.K., 1990), p. 248.
[2]Ibid., p. 25.
[3]Tony Campolo, "Getting out of the World Alive," *Discipleship Journal*, no. 86 (1995): 46.

Chapter 4: Dangerous Question #1: Who Is Jesus?
[1]J. Robertson McQuilkin, *The Great Omission* (Grand Rapids, Mich.: Baker Book House, 1984), p. 41.
[2]Ibid., p. 42.
[3]James Davison Hunter, *Evangelicalism: The Coming Generation* (Chicago: University of Chicago Press, 1987), p. 35.
[4]Peter Cotterell, *Mission and Meaninglessness* (London: S.P.C.K., 1990), p. 56.
[5]Craig Blomberg, *The Historical Reliability of the Gospels* (Downers Grove, Ill.: InterVarsity Press, 1987), p. 77.
[6]Cotterell, *Mission and Meaninglessness*, p. 263.
[7]McQuilkin, *Great Omission*, pp. 50-51.
[8]Harold Lindsell, *An Evangelical Theology of Missions* (Grand Rapids, Mich.: Zondervan, 1970), p. 113.
[9]Quoted in Courtney Anderson, *To the Golden Shore* (Valley Forge, Penn.: Judson Press, 1987), p. 83.

[10]Ajith Fernando, *The Supremacy of Christ* (Wheaton, Ill.: Crossway, 1995), p. 103.
[11]Ibid., p. 262.
[12]C. S. Lewis, *Mere Christianity* (New York: Macmillan, 1972), p. 56.

Chapter 5: Dangerous Question #2: Do I Believe in Heaven?
[1]Bernie May, sermon given at Black Rock Congregational Church, Fairfield, Connecticut, November 18, 1995.
[2]Tony Campolo, *Wake Up America!* (Grand Rapids, Mich.: HarperCollins/Zondervan, 1991), p. 7.
[3]George G. Hunter III, *How to Reach Secular People* (Nashville: Abingdon, 1992), p. 45.
[4]Steve Chalke, lecture presented at Brainstormers Conference, Blackpool, England, November 11, 1995.
[5]Bob Seiple, "Send Them Home with Horses," lecture presented to the U.S. secretary of state's Open Forum, September 13, 1995; quote is from p. 3 of the published version (Seattle: World Vision, 1995).
[6]Philip Yancey, "Why Not Now?" *Christianity Today,* February 5, 1996, p. 112.
[7]Seiple, "Send Them Home with Horses," p. 9.
[8]Michael Griffiths, *Give Up Your Small Ambitions* (Chicago: Moody Press, 1973), p. 78.

Chapter 6: Dangerous Question #3: Do I Believe in Hell?
[1]Ajith Fernando, *Crucial Questions About Hell* (Eastbourne, U.K.: Kingsway, 1991), p. 169.
[2]Peter Cotterell, *Mission and Meaninglessness* (London: S.P.C.K., 1995), p. 27.
[3]Norman Geisler, "Everything You Wanted to Know About Heaven but Were Afraid to Ask," *Discipleship Journal,* no. 87 (1995): 31-35.
[4]Ibid., p. 32.
[5]Fernando, *Crucial Questions About Hell*, p. 134.
[6]John Stott and David Edwards, *Evangelical Essentials* (Downers Grove, Ill.: InterVarsity Press, 1988), p. 292.
[7]Cotterell, *Mission and Meaninglessness*, p. 73.
[8]Ibid., p. 74.
[9]Fernando, *Crucial Questions About Hell*, p. 150.
[10]Stott and Edwards, *Evangelical Essentials*, p. 312.

Chapter 7: Dangerous Question #4: Does Christianity Matter?
[1]Peter Cotterell, *Mission and Meaninglessness* (London: S.P.C.K., 1990), p. 173.
[2]Stephen Neill, *Crises of Belief* (London: Hodder & Stoughton, 1948), p. 248.
[3]George G. Hunter III, *How to Reach Secular People* (Nashville: Abingdon, 1992), p. 48.
[4]Luis Palau, "Only the Gospel Can Change America," *Discipleship Journal,* no. 86 (1995): 41.

[5]Hunter, *How to Reach Secular People*, p. 112.
[6]Bob Lupton, *Urban Perspectives* newsletter, June 1994.
[7]John Stott, *Involvement*, 2 vols. (Old Tappan, N.J.: Revell, 1985).
[8]Lesslie Newbigin, *The Gospel in a Pluralist Society* (Grand Rapids, Mich.: Eerdmans, 1989), p. 101.
[9]Vincent Donovan, *Christianity Rediscovered* (Maryknoll, N.Y.: Orbis, 1978), p. 78.

Chapter 8: Dangerous Question #5: Do I Believe That God Wants to Use My Life?

[1]Ted Engstrom, *Motivation to Last a Lifetime* (Grand Rapids, Mich.: Zondervan, 1984), p. 30.

Chapter 9: Dangerous Question #6: Whose Agenda Will I Live By?

[1]Howard Snyder, *A Kingdom Manifesto* (Downers Grove, Ill.: InterVarsity Press, 1985), p. 111.
[2]Robert Coleman, *The Great Commission Life-Style* (Old Tappan, N.J.: Revell, 1992), p. 34.
[3]J. Robertson McQuilkin, *The Great Omission* (Grand Rapids, Mich.: Baker Book House, 1985), p. 73.
[4]Ibid.
[5]Michael Griffiths, *Give Up Your Small Ambitions* (Chicago: Moody Press, 1973), p. 6.
[6]Tony Campolo, "Getting out of the World Alive," *Discipleship Journal*, no. 86 (1995): 45.

Chapter 10: How's Your Worldview?

[1]Bob Seiple, general circulation letter dated November 1, 1995.
[2]Peter Kuzmic, installation sermon at Gordon-Conwell Theological Seminary, September 9, 1994.